THEMED BABY SHOWERS

From Mother Goose to Noah's Ark, Hundreds of Creative Shower Ideas

Becky Long

Meadowbrook Press

Distributed by Simon & Schuster
New York

Library of Congress Cataloging-in-Publication Data
Long, Becky.
  Themed baby showers : from Mother Goose to Noah's ark hundreds of
creative shower ideas / by Becky Long.
      p. cm.
  ISBN 0-88166-436-7 (Meadowbrook)   ISBN 0-684-01871-3 (Simon & Schuster)
  1. Showers (Parties) 2. Entertaining. I. Title.
  GV1472.7.S5 L66 2003
  793.2—dc21
                                    2002152799

Editorial Director: Christine Zuchora-Walske
Editor: Megan McGinnis
Proofreader: Angela Wiechmann
Production Manager: Paul Woods
Graphic Design Manager: Tamara Peterson
Art Director: Peggy Bates
Cover Art and Illustrations: Joyce Shelton
Technical Illustrations and Templates: Tamara Peterson

Published by Meadowbrook Press, 5451 Smetana Drive, Minnetonka, Minnesota 55343

www.meadowbrookpress.com

BOOK TRADE DISTRIBUTION by Simon and Schuster, a division of Simon and
Schuster, Inc., 1230 Avenue of the Americas, New York, NY 10020

08 07 06 05 04   10 9 8 7 6 5 4 3 2

Printed in the United States of America

Dedication
This book is dedicated to
Cayman and Moorea—the babies
who've showered my world with happiness.
And to Mom—my inspiration!

Acknowledgments
Much like having a baby, writing this book was a
labor of love. It's delivery was nurtured by the special efforts of
Julie Day, Melissa Crawford, Kim Queen, Amy Hastert, Kathy Lovig,
Opal Morris, Dr. Eric Peck, Dr. Charles Powell, and the outstanding
team at Meadowbrook Press—especially Megan McGinnis,
Christine Zuchora-Walske, and Bruce Lansky.

In addition, Meadowbrook Press and I thank the
following women for reviewing the early stages of this book:
Maija Freivalds, Jenni Lawrence, O. J. Magnan, Cindy Miller,
Jeanne Schuller, Tanya Silver, Jana Sullivan, Danielle
White, Angie Wiechmann, and Dina Wren.

CONTENTS

INTRODUCTION

Would you like to host a baby shower that really packs pizzazz? If so, you're holding the perfect book in your hands. *Themed Baby Showers* is bursting with simple yet sensational party ideas guaranteed to make your next baby shower extraordinary. Each of the unique shower themes is spelled out from start to finish and couldn't be easier to carry out.

Time is precious. Guests don't often jump at the chance to give up a Saturday afternoon to drink punch and play goofy games that stifle conversation, insult their intelligence, and do little to celebrate the arrival of a bundle of joy. This book breathes new life into the time-honored tradition of baby showers. In it you'll find imaginative invitations that'll have your guests eagerly anticipating the party. You'll learn how to wow guests with dazzling decorations, fabulous foods, and exceptional entertainment that'll leave them clamoring for more. You'll discover great gift ideas for the baby and mom-to-be, as well as fun favor ideas for the guests. With this book as your guide, your toughest job will be getting the guests to go home when the party's over!

This book also provides delightful party plans for hosting a couples' shower, an open house celebration after the baby is born, a shower by mail for a faraway friend, a scaled-down "sprinkle" for a friend who's had the full shower experience, and a shower that spotlights the expectant sibling.

A new life is truly something to celebrate, so do just that and do it with style. You and your guests are about to have a whole lot of fun!

The Top Ten Tasks That Need to Get Done

1. Share your desire to throw a shower with the mom-to-be—that is, if you're not planning on surprising her. (Keep in mind, though, a surprise shower may not be appreciated by someone with frequent doctor's appointments, sleepless nights, and swollen ankles.) Get a clear picture from her about what would make the celebration special. Ask her for a guest list and any requests.

2. Give your party personality. Is there a party theme that intrigues you or fits the mom-to-be's quirky sense of humor? Or perhaps there's a special activity you'd like to incorporate. Brainstorm ideas and select which ones you'll use after you've determined the budget and the guest list.

3. Set a date for the celebration. Keep in mind holidays and other potential date conflicts to encourage a good turnout. Discuss with the mom-to-be whether she'd like to have the shower before or after the baby is born. (If the shower's a surprise, use one of the following schedules.) If she opts for a shower before the birth, be sure to schedule the party at least four to six weeks before baby's scheduled arrival. (Keep in mind that a mom-to-be expecting multiples may mean an even earlier arrival.) If the mom-to-be decides to have the shower after the baby's birth, tentatively set the party date for at least one month after the baby's due date. This scheduling will accommodate a baby that might arrive late, and will give both mom and baby a moment to settle into their new routine. Wait to mail the invitations and confirm party details until after the baby is born.

4. Set a budget. Determine your priorities and limitations. Talk openly about these decisions with any cohosts.

5. Assemble the guest list. This list affects everything from your party venue to the number of forks you'll need. If you already have a venue in mind for the celebration, note its space limitations and share those with the mom-to-be if she's helping you

come up with a guest list. If the shower is a surprise, ask for input from someone close to the mom-to-be.

6. Secure the venue. Make necessary arrangements to accommodate the party, like chair or other equipment rentals.

7. Start searching for party goods, like plates and decorations. The earlier your hunt begins, the more likely you'll find just what you're looking for.

8. Plan the menu. Each party in this book offers great recipes for wonderful theme-related foods, but remember to select a menu that won't stretch your culinary skills. If appropriate, choose no-fuss foods that you can make ahead of time and that won't require much last-minute preparation. Also keep in mind your available oven, refrigerator, and freezer space. Finally, if you don't have enough table space to seat guests, serve food they can easily eat from small plates balanced on their laps.

9. Prepare the invitations. Be sure to include the shower date, time, and location. Give a date by which you'd like guests to RSVP and provide a phone number for them to call with their responses. Also enclose any special instructions specific to your party theme. For example, if you've chosen to host a surprise shower, enclose a few pink and blue jellybeans along with a note that reads, "Shhh…it's a surprise. Don't spill the beans." You may choose to enclose gift registry information as well.

10. After you've checked off every task on your list, relax! If you're having a good time, your guests will, too. If some things don't go according to plan, just let them go. (You're probably the only one who noticed anyway!)

The Top Five Time and Money Savers

1. Find a cohost or two, and you've potentially cut your costs by a half or a third.

2. Keep the numbers in check. While certain costs are fixed and not affected by the headcount (like decorations), many costs are directly proportional to the number of guests (like food). Call guests who haven't responded to ensure less goes to waste.

3. Shop early. The more time you have to find clearance sales of party supplies, the better your odds of finding them. Also check online auction sites for bargains and browse thrift shops for decorations.

4. Schedule your celebration for midmorning or midafternoon when a light menu can be served.

5. Choose theme ideas that can serve a dual purpose. For example, choose favors that can double as decorations, such as chocolate kiss rosebud favors that can become a beautiful centerpiece when placed in a vase (see page 75).

The Perfect Party Checklist

After you've planned your party from start to finish, use the following checklist to help you organize and track the preparations. You may want to photocopy the list and carry it with you, checking off tasks as you complete them. Note some tasks may not apply to your particular party plan. Feel free to add any tasks specific to your celebration. The better planned and organized you are, the more of a smashing success your party will be.

At least three months before the party

❏ Call the mom-to-be to discuss a date and time for the celebration.

❏ Brainstorm the party's style or theme.

❏ Set a budget.

❏ Formulate a preliminary guest list with mailing addresses and phone numbers.

❏ Secure a venue.

❏ Plan entertainment and activities.

❏ Hire a caterer if necessary.

At least two months before the party

❏ Confirm the guest list.

❏ Select or design invitations.

❏ Assemble favorite recipes. Place food orders or confirm caterer's menu.

At least one month before the party

❏ Prepare and mail the invitations. Include any special instructions or directions to the party site.

❏ Select the decorations.

❏ Buy or make the perfect gift.

❏ Reserve any necessary rentals, like food service items or chairs.

One week before the party

❏ Review the invitation responses to determine the final headcount.

❏ Secure necessary prizes and materials for scheduled activities.

❏ Gather linens, china, and flatware. Or purchase disposable table service.

❏ Prepare party favors, name tags, place cards, and seating chart.

❏ Buy film, if necessary.

❏ Finalize the menu and create a shopping list for ingredients.

❏ Confirm rentals, orders, or hired services with reminder phone calls.

Two days before the party

❏ Wrap your gift.

❏ Purchase necessary food items.

❏ Prepare any make-ahead dishes.

❏ Locate necessary serving dishes and utensils.

❏ Rearrange furniture. Set up tables and chairs.

❏ Decorate the party venue with everything except balloons and streamers.

The day of the party

❏ Prepare last-minute menu items and remove any premade entrées from the freezer, including the punch.

❏ Inflate balloons and complete decorations.

❏ Place fresh hand towels in the bathroom and make sure there's plenty of toilet paper.

❏ Have pen and paper handy to log gifts and a trash bag nearby to collect gift-wrap.

❏ Dress at least one hour before the party is scheduled to begin.

❏ Create ambience by lighting candles and turning on music to welcome guests.

❏ Have fun!

Party Formula

Here's a tested party formula that works well at any baby shower. Make changes to the itinerary to best suit your needs. Watch your guests closely for signs that they're ready to move on to the next step and adapt the schedule accordingly.

1. Greet guests.
2. Make introductions.
3. Play an icebreaker activity to get guests mingling.
4. Follow with the main activity.
5. Eat food.
6. Open gifts.
7. Eat the dessert.
8. Pass out favors.
9. Thank guests for attending.
10. Help the mom-to-be pack up her treasures.

SHOWER THEMES

A theme can provide the framework for your party and is almost certain to make your celebration more enjoyable. Your shower plans could center on your extraordinary collection of teddy bears or the mom-to-be's immense passion for gardening. Or maybe the décor that's planned for the baby's nursery is all the party inspiration you'll need.

What follows are fifteen wonderful themed parties designed to help you celebrate baby's arrival in grand style. To get the most from this book, please read each of the themes in their broadest of terms, noting that many of the ideas found in each theme can be used or adapted for other themes. And remember to look for ways to add your own creative touches. After all, the shower won't be unique if you don't make your mark on it!

STORK SHOWER

Here's a salute to the long-legged friends that have long been associated with baby's arrival.

Invitations

→ Use stork eggs (plastic Easter eggs) to invite the guests. Enclose party details in the eggs and mail them in small boxes.

→ Use the stork template on page 121 to cut stork-shaped invitations from white card stock. Decorate the cutouts with colored markers and glued-on white feathers. (You can buy feathers at a craft supply store.) If desired, glue on chenille stems for legs. Write party details on the baby sling. Punch a hole through the stork's beak and attach the baby sling with ribbon. Mail the invitations in vellum envelopes.

→ Stick a feather in each envelope along with the invitation that includes the party details and this poem:

> *Soon the stork will make a stop.*
> *Our dear friend is going to "pop."*
> *Won't you come and celebrate?*
> *We'll have fun, so don't be late!*

Decorations

→ Glue a tiny plastic baby into a small bird's nest. (You can buy artificial nests at a craft supply store.) Glue the nest near the bottom of a twig wreath. Attach other baby items, like newborn socks and teething rings, to the wreath with floral wire. Hang the wreath on the front door along with a banner that reads "[mom-to-be's name] Is Nesting!" Give the wreath to the guest of honor when the party is over.

Stork Egg Invitations

Stork Invitations

Stork Feather Invitations

Nesting Wreath

→ Use the stork template on page 121 to cut a stork centerpiece from foam board. (Photocopy the template to enlarge as needed.) Decorate the stork using colored markers, paint, and/or glued-on white feathers. Write best wishes to the mom-to-be on the baby sling and attach the sling to the beak with ribbon. Prop the stork between two bricks placed in a twig wreath to resemble a nest. Cover the bricks with a baby blanket, fabric, or paper shreds.

→ Decorate a buffet table with nests made from long pasta in a variety of colors. The night before the party, cook then drain the pasta. While the noodles are soft, mold them into nest shapes large enough to hold an egg. Allow the nests to harden on wax paper overnight. Fill the nests with hard-boiled eggs dyed in shades of pink and blue or any color you choose.

Activities

→ Play Stork Gift Bingo. Make copies of the game card on page 119. As guests arrive, instruct them to write in the squares of the game cards the names of shower gifts they think the mom-to-be will likely receive (for example, hooded towels, pajamas, and blankets for baby). They may write a gift name in more than one square, but only one square may be marked per gift opened. At the gift opening, give each guest twenty-five jelly-beans. As the mom-to-be unwraps each gift, guests mark the corresponding squares on their cards. If there isn't enough table-top space to keep the game cards level, have guests mark their card squares with stickers or crayons. A player should yell "Stork!" when she fills all of the squares in a vertical, horizontal, or diagonal line on her card. If you need to break a tie between two winners, award the prize to the player whose birthday is closest to the baby's due date.

→ Write baby-related charades, truth-or-consequences questions, or a combination of both on separate slips of paper. For the charades, see Baby Doodles on page 130 for inspiration. For the questions, write questions that will test the guests' knowledge

Stork Centerpiece

❧

Stork Nests

❧

Stork Gift Bingo

❧

*Baby Charades/
Truth or Consequences*

about the mom-to-be's pregnancy, childhood, or plans for the nursery, and also include consequences, such as "Put a quarter in the baby's piggy bank." (Get the correct answers from the mom-to-be prior to the party, and write them on a sheet of paper.) Put the slips in separate plastic eggs and hide them around the party area before the shower. When it's time to play the game, tell guests the eggs contain prizes so they'll hunt for as many eggs as possible. Tell them not to open the eggs until all the eggs have been found. When the hunt is over, the guests will be surprised to discover the true contents of the eggs. Have guests take turns opening their eggs and performing the tasks on the slips. If a guest correctly identifies a charade being acted out, the actor and the guesser each earns a point. If a guest correctly answers a question, then she earns a point. If she answers incorrectly, then she must pay the consequence. Award a prize to the guest with the most points.

→ Put guests to the test with Mr. Stork's Special Delivery Quiz (see page 124). They'll have to know a lot more than where babies come from to ace this quiz!

Gifts

→ Invite guests to bring their gifts wrapped in receiving blankets or towels rather than gift-wrap. Make a large stork's nest from crumbled brown craft paper. Gather twigs and buy white feathers from your local craft store, and stick the items into the paper nest. House the gift bundles in the nest.

→ To help the mom-to-be prepare her nest for baby, invite each guest to bring a small gift that fits into a large Easter egg, such as a pacifier, baby nail clippers, coupons, or gift certificates. Give each guest an Easter egg upon arrival, ask her to put her small gift inside the egg, and present all the eggs in a basket to the guest of honor.

→ Take the stork template on page 121 to a copy store and enlarge the template so you can make a large door or yard sign from cardboard. The mom-to-be can post the sign when baby has arrived. Leave space on the sign for her to write baby's birth stats in pink or blue.

Stork Sign

Favors

→ Wrap scented votive candles in tulle. Choose appropriate colors if you know the sex of the baby. You may also use clean glass baby food jars as candleholders. For each candle, attach a decorative tag that features the following poetic lines:

> *After the stork brings me in flight,*
> *Make a wish by candlelight.*

Baby Jar Candles

→ Thanks to their egg shape, Jordan almonds might be the perfect favor for you. Fill small bags with almonds, and to each bag attach a decorative tag that reads, "Miniature stork eggs to thank you for such an 'eggciting' afternoon!" Display the favors in a stork's nest (see Stork Centerpiece on page 11).

Miniature Stork Eggs

→ Buy small papier-mâché boxes from your local craft store. Paint the boxes pink or blue. Coil raffia into bird's nest shapes and set a nest in each box. Place jellybeans or foil-wrapped chocolate eggs in each nest along with a note of thanks.

Stork Eggs in a Box

Food

→ Serve fruit and cheese kabobs on stork skewers. Follow these instructions to make each stork skewer:

1 diaper pin with plain white head
1¼-inch toothpick piece
Two 5-millimeter googly eyes
Four 6-inch strands of curling ribbon
Glue
Scissors

Stork Skewer
Kabobs

Halfway down the attached side of the diaper pin, bend the metal ninety degrees away from the pinhead (see illustration). Glue a googly eye onto each side of the pinhead, and create a beak by gluing the toothpick piece into the pinhead. Tie curling ribbon to the hole at the stork's tail.

→ Serve pasta nests. Prepare your favorite long-noodle pasta recipe. Form the noodles into nest shapes in separate bowls. Nestle baby scallops or meatballs in each nest. Perch a plastic stork on each bowl's edge for a whimsical touch.

→ Stork Nest Dessert Cups
2 cups miniature marshmallows
¼ cup butter
6-ounce package chow mein noodles
Pink or blue Jordan almonds

Melt the marshmallows and butter over low heat in a 2-quart saucepan. Add the chow mein noodles to the mixture and stir until they're well coated. Using a greased 12-cup muffin pan, form nests by pressing the mixture onto the bottom and sides of each cup. Refrigerate the nests for 3 hours or until firm. Remove the nests from the cups and fill them with Jordan almonds.

→ Stork Cake
Two 9-inch round cakes and one 13-by-9-inch cake, cooled
    (Prepare the cakes from packaged mixes or double the recipe
    on page 115 to make all 3 cakes.)
Three 16-ounce cans white frosting (Use the recipe on page 115
    to make your own.)
Yellow and red food coloring
1 large marshmallow
1 blue M&M
Fabric baby sling

Carefully remove the cakes from the pans. Wrap each cake in plastic wrap and freeze the cakes for 1 hour to make for easier cutting and fewer crumbs. Remove the plastic wrap from the cakes. Cut the cakes as shown below and place the pieces on a cake board that measures at least 32-by-22 inches. Mix yellow and red food coloring into 2 cups of frosting, and use the orange frosting to color the stork's beak, legs, and feet. Decorate the rest of the stork's body with white frosting. To make the eye, cut the marshmallow in half and nestle the M&M into the top of one half. Set the eye in place on the stork's head. Complete the cake by positioning a fabric baby sling from the stork's beak. This recipe makes 24 servings.

Stork Cake

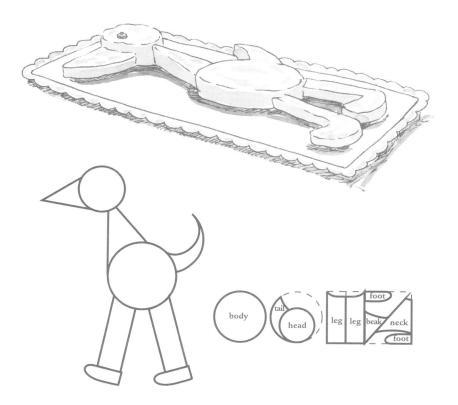

Mother Goose Parade

Base your baby shower on a classic collection of nursery rhymes, and you're sure to receive rave reviews.

Invitations

→ Write the party details on small note cards and tuck the note cards into pocketsize copies of *Mother Goose*. Or make Mother Goose book covers from card stock and pen party details inside.

→ Write the following caption along with party details on decorative paper plates: "Hey, diddle, diddle! Come celebrate [mom-to-be's name]'s middle!" Use a hole punch and ribbon to attach a plastic spoon to each plate. Mail the invitations in padded envelopes.

→ Pour clean, crushed eggshells into vellum envelopes. Decorate egg shapes cut from card stock to look like Humpty Dumpty. Write party details and the rhyme about Humpty Dumpty on the back of each egg invitation.

Decorations

→ If weather permits, host the party outdoors in Mary, Mary, Quite Contrary's garden. Add imaginative touches, like taper candles set in candlesticks for Jack Be Nimble, Jack Be Quick; stars cut from card stock and covered with aluminum foil for Twinkle, Twinkle, Little Star; and a baby doll set in a light-weight toy cradle hanging from a tree branch for Rock-a-Bye, Baby. Make a Jack and Jill wishing well by wrapping a small clothes hamper with brown or red paper. Draw a brick pattern all over the paper. Set the well on a large box or two and cover the boxes with green fabric to make the hill.

Mother Goose
Book Invitations

Hey, Diddle, Diddle!
Invitations

Humpty Dumpty
Invitations

Mary, Mary, Quite
Contrary's Garden Setting

→ For unique place settings, attach plates and spoons together with decorative ribbon and tape. Attach to each place setting a tag card that reads, "And the dish ran away with the spoon!" For a coordinating centerpiece, write the same phrase with a dry-erase marker on a large colorful ceramic plate and place the plate on an easel.

Dish & Spoon Table Setting

→ Have Mother Goose grace your party scene. Cut a large goose shape from white card stock and add details with markers or paints. Or use a large plush goose or garden goose statue. Tie a big hat to the head with a long scarf and prop copies of *Mother Goose* around the feet. Have each guest pen a short rhyme to the baby on the inside cover of one of the books.

Mother Goose Figure

Activities

→ As an icebreaker, write the names of nursery rhyme characters on separate slips of paper and attach a slip to each guest's back upon arrival. Challenge the guests to learn the names on their backs by asking yes-or-no questions to the other guests. Award a prize to the last person to learn her nursery rhyme identity.

Mother Goose Identity Game

→ Play Mother Goose Rhetoric. Photocopy the game sheet on page 125 as needed. At game time, distribute the game sheets and pencils, and set the timer for five minutes. Challenge players to write down the first line of the nursery rhyme alluded to by each phrase. The player who gets the most correct in the least amount of time is the winner. Award prizes that correspond to the rhymes, such as a pie pan for Little Jack Horner or a pair of mittens for the Three Little Kittens.

Mother Goose Rhetoric

→ Make a felt storyboard for the future toddler. Provide wool felt in assorted colors along with scissors, glue, markers, fabric paints, and any embellishments that aren't choking hazards to toddlers. Guests can cut beloved nursery rhyme characters and props from the felt. To make the task easier, provide a copy of *Mother Goose* with good illustrations that guests may trace and

Mother Goose Storyboard

Mother Goose Storyboard

Nursery Rhyme Gifts

Stock the Cupboard

Fill the Well

Hot Cross Buns

*Mary, Mary, Quite
Contrary Flower Bulbs*

use as patterns. You can buy a felt storyboard on which the figures can tell a story, or craft one by gluing felt (sky blue is a good color) onto the inside lid of a shoebox. The figures will stick to the backdrop for hours of storytelling fun and can be stored in the shoebox. If you like, decorate the outside of the shoebox as well.

Gifts

→ In the invitations, assign each guest a nursery rhyme and request she bring a gift that corresponds. For example, "Wee Willie Winkie" could mean a sleeper for baby, "Rub-a-Dub-Dub" might yield baby bath goodies, and "Mary, Mary, Quite Contrary" might equal a growth chart. Suggest guests wrap their gifts to look like nursery rhyme books. Award a prize for the most creative gift-wrapping.

→ Don't let the mom-to-be become Old Mother Hubbard. In the invitations, ask guests to help stock the mom-to-be's cupboard with jars of baby food. Place the items in the Jack and Jill wishing well (see Mary, Mary, Quite Contrary's Garden Setting on page 16).

→ Or invite guests to fill the wishing well with inexpensive baby products. Give the products to the mom-to-be or donate them to a local women's or homeless shelter.

Favors

→ Individually wrap Hot Cross Buns (buy or make the buns) in cellophane and ribbon. Attach to each bun a tag card that features the nursery rhyme and a note that reads, "Thank you from [mom-to-be's name]'s little bun in the oven."

→ In honor of Mary, Mary, Quite Contrary, send guests home with flower bulbs in pyramid favor boxes (see page 120).

Food

→ For fun, write as many different nursery rhymes on note cards as the number of guests you expect. Cut each note card at the middle of each rhyme. Seat guests by giving each the first half of a nursery rhyme and having her find the rest of the rhyme at a place setting.

→ Link menu items to nursery rhymes. Place deviled eggs on a platter, set a brick on the center of the platter, and perch a toy Humpty Dumpty on the brick. Salute Mary, Mary, Quite Contrary with a vegetable tray and the man that lives on Drury Lane with a basket of muffins. Serve punch in a galvanized bucket for Jack and Jill, and hot tea for Polly Put the Kettle On.

→ Old Woman in the Shoe Cake

Two 9-by-5-inch cakes, cooled (Prepare the cakes from a packaged mix or use the recipe on page 115.)
Two 16-ounce cans white frosting (Use the recipe on page 115 to make your own.)
Chocolate wafer cookies
Tube of brown frosting
Cinnamon candies
Red licorice
Chocolate graham crackers

Carefully remove the cakes from the pans. Wrap the cakes in plastic wrap and freeze them for 1 hour to make for easier cutting and fewer crumbs. Remove the plastic wrap, then level the tops and sides of both cakes. Lay one cake on a cake board and stand the other cake upright next to one end of the horizontal cake. Bevel the top of the upright cake on both sides to make a rooftop. Round the free end of the horizontal cake to form the front of the shoe. Cover both cakes with white frosting. Use chocolate wafer cookies to form roof shingles. Squeeze brown frosting around the bottom edge of the shoe to form the sole.

Nursery Rhyme Place Settings

❦

Nursery Rhyme Buffet

❦

Old Woman in the Shoe Cake

*Old Woman
in the Shoe Cake*

Pat-a-Cake

Use cinnamon candies and licorice to lace the shoe. Stick on a chocolate graham cracker door and window. Add frosting windowpanes and doorknob. Stand toy children around the cake. This recipe makes 16 servings.

→ If you're short on time, you can make a Pat-a-Cake by baking a sheet cake and marking it with a frosting *B*.

PEA IN THE POD: A GARDEN PARTY

This garden shower is sure to yield a bumper crop of compliments.

Invitations

→ Write party details on small note cards along with the heading "There's a pea in [mom-to-be's name]'s pod." Glue the note cards onto separate packets of pea seeds. Write "hand cancel" on the mailing envelopes to prevent the seed invitations from getting crushed in postal machinery.

→ Cut pea pod shapes from green card stock using the template on page 118. For each pea pod, write party details on one side. Glue green glitter or craft stone "peas" down the center of the other side. Mail in padded envelopes.

→ Use a fine-tip permanent marker to print party details on inexpensive plain garden gloves. If only patterned gloves are available, write the party details on card stock and insert the invitations in the garden gloves. Mail the gloves in large envelopes.

Decorations

→ Gather pillar candles and use them to make a unique centerpiece. Decorate the candles with candle rings made from strings of sugar snap peas. For each candle, use a large needle to thread the pea pods onto a raffia strand. When you reach the desired length, tie the pea pods around the base of the candle along with a decorative tag that reads, "Celebrating the Pea in the Pod."

Pea Seeds Invitations

❦

Pea Pod Invitations

❦

Garden Glove Invitations

❦

Pea Pod Candles

Diaper Banner

→ Paint or machine-embroider "baby shower" on cloth diapers (one letter per diaper). Or use colorful markers to write the words on disposable diapers. Hang the diapers from a ribbon clothesline. When the baby arrives, the mom-to-be can put the diapers to good use on baby's bottom or as burp cloths. If you like, have extra clothespins on hand to hang any baby garments that are given as gifts.

Pea Pod Centerpieces

→ Create pea pod wall hangings or centerpieces from green felt and balloons. Enlarge the pea pod template on page 118 to the desired size and use it to cut pea pod shapes from the felt. Inflate the balloon "peas" and tape them in place on the shapes. Attach curled chenille stems for tendrils.

Birth Flower Decorations

→ Incorporate the baby's birth flowers into your decorations. Here's the list of birth flowers:

January: carnation or snowdrop
February: violet or primrose
March: jonquil or violet
April: daisy or sweet pea
May: lily of the valley or hawthorn
June: rose or honeysuckle
July: larkspur or water lily
August: poppy or gladiolus
September: aster or morning glory
October: calendula or marigold
November: chrysanthemum
December: narcissus or holly

Place the flowers in vases carved from cleaned-out watermelons.

Babies in Pots

→ Cut out Anne Geddes prints of babies dressed as flowers to enhance your shower décor. Glue the cutouts onto Popsicle sticks, and stick them in flower pots filled with florist's foam so babies can be found "growing" everywhere.

Activities

→ Play Name That Baby Food. Buy eight jars of baby fruits or vegetables. Cover each jar's label with paper and number each jar. To play, give each player a paper plate, a spoon, and a pencil. Ask her to write the numbers 1 to 8 around the rim of the plate. Stick a baby spoon in each jar, and have the players pass the first jar around and place a spoonful of its contents near the number 1 on their plates. Repeat this process for the remaining seven jars. At your mark, have the players taste each food and write down what they think the food is near the corresponding number. Award a can of vegetables to the player who identifies the most food correctly. To make the game more challenging, choose foods that combine more than one type of fruit or vegetable.

→ Play Pass the Produce. Buy twenty different produce items, like a pea pod, a carrot, an ear of corn, and so on. To play, seat players in a close circle with their hands behind their backs. Set one item in a player's hands and ask her to feel it then pass it on to the next player, who will feel the item and pass it on to the next player, and so on around the circle. When the first player has passed an item on, give her the next item to feel. Continue this process until you've given the first player all twenty items. When an item has made its way around the circle, take it and place it in a paper bag so it won't make another round. When all the items have been felt, give the players paper and pencils and challenge them to write down the items in the order they were passed. (Make sure you know the order before you pass the items out!) Award a bag of frozen peas to the player who comes closest to listing the items in the correct order.

→ Make a keepsake garden stone for the mom-to-be to commemorate this special day. Kits are available at your local craft store. Have each guest place a small decorative stone in the cement while offering a special wish to baby.

Name That Baby Food

❦

Pass the Produce

❦

Keepsake Garden Stone

Garden Gifts

Perennial Presents

Fill the Flower Pot

Flower Bulb Bundles

Baby Photo Plant Stakes

Gifts

→ In the invitations, assign each guest a different item found in the garden and ask her to bring a gift that corresponds. For example, for a green bean one might choose to give baby a green outfit and a copy of *Jack and the Beanstalk.*

→ Indulge baby with perennial presents. Assign a different month or season to each guest and request that they bring a gift that relates to that time of year. Incorporate the sports seasons if the mom-to-be is an avid sports fan.

→ Invite guests to bring food items that will help baby grow. (Remind guests to note expiration dates on jars of baby food. Baby will not be able to eat these items for a few months.) Have them deposit their food gifts in a large flower pot. If the mom-to-be likes, donate the food items to a local women's or homeless shelter in the baby's name.

Favors

→ Give guests flower bulbs wrapped in tulle and tied with pink and blue ribbon. On gift tags, write "May [mom-to-be's name]'s shower bring you flowers. Thanks for coming!" Attach each tag to a bundle of bulbs. Or place the bulbs in pyramid favor boxes (see page 120).

→ If the shower will take place after the baby's birth, give each guest a small potted plant complete with a photo of the baby on a plant stake. To make the plant stakes, glue laminated photos of baby onto Popsicle sticks. Write baby's statistics on tag cards and attach a card to each pot.

Food

→ Serve food in decorative wheelbarrows and flowerpots. Identify menu items on plant stakes made from card stock and Popsicle sticks.

→ Make flower ice cubes. Fill each section of an ice cube tray halfway with cold water and freeze until solid. Place a small edible flower or flower petal in each section. (Make sure the flowers are clean, dry, and pesticide free. Try bright blue borage flowers or Johnny-jump-ups. Other edible varieties include roses, nasturtiums, pansies, carnations, and chrysanthemums.) Fill the sections with water, and freeze again until serving.

→ Peas in the Pod

Fresh sweet pea pods
8-ounce package veggie-flavored cream cheese, softened
Frozen green peas, thawed

Slit the seam of each pea pod with a knife. Use a pastry bag (or see page 116 to make your own pastry bag) to fill the pea pods with cream cheese. Top each pea pod with three peas. Serve the pea pods on a platter.

→ Lay veggies on a tray in a wreath shape. Start with larger produce, like broccoli florets, and fill in gaps with smaller items like baby carrots and cauliflower pieces. If necessary, use toothpicks to secure the foods. Serve your favorite vegetable dip in a wax-paper-lined terra cotta pot placed in the center of the veggie wreath.

→ Dirt Pie

8-ounce package cream cheese, softened
1 stick butter or margarine, melted
Two 3.9-ounce boxes instant vanilla pudding mix
3½ cups milk
16-ounce container frozen whipped topping, thawed
1¼ pound package Oreo cookies, finely crushed
Gummi worms

Garden Buffet Accessories

❦

Flower Ice Cubes

❦

Peas in the Pod

❦

Veggie Wreath

❦

Dirt Pie

Dirt Pie

Pea Pod Cake

Line a terra cotta flowerpot with wax paper. Mix the first 5 ingredients together in a bowl. Alternate layering this mixture with a layer of crushed Oreo "dirt." Be certain to end with a "dirt" layer. Top the pie with an artificial flower and drape Gummi worms over the side of the pot. Use a garden trowel to serve the pie. This recipe makes 20 servings.

→ Pea Pod Cake

Batter to make one 13-by-9-inch cake (Prepare the batter from a packaged mix or use the recipe on page 115.)

Two 16-ounce cans white frosting (Use the recipe on page 115 to make your own.)

Green food coloring
Green sugar sprinkles

Place 3 cupcake liners in a muffin pan. Pour the cake batter into the liners, filling each only halfway. Pour the remaining batter into a greased cake pan. Bake the cakes according to package or recipe instructions. Allow the cakes to cool, then carefully remove the sheet cake from the pan. Wrap the sheet cake with plastic wrap and freeze it for 1 hour to make for easier cutting and fewer crumbs. Enlarge the pea pod template on page 118 and use it to cut a pea pod shape from the sheet cake (remove the plastic wrap first). Place the cake cutout on a cake board. Tint the frosting light green and use it to frost the cake cutout and cupcakes. Set the cupcake peas in place on the cake pea pod and add frosting tendrils. Cover the cupcake peas with green sugar sprinkles. This recipe makes 9 servings.

PITTER PATTER, PAT-A-CAKE

This delightful shower salutes baby's hands and feet. You're sure to get a "thumbs up" from all who attend.

Invitations

→ Cut baby footprint shapes from pink or blue card stock. Write party details on the cutouts and insert them into separate newborn socks. Mail the invitations in padded envelopes decorated with baby footprints. To make the footprints, dip your fist sideways (pinkie side down) into paint or press it onto an ink pad, then press it onto the envelope. Use your right fist to create a right foot and your left fist to create a left foot. Add toes by dipping your fingertips into paint and pressing them in place.

Baby Footprints Invitations

🐣

→ Cut handprint shapes from beautiful handmade paper (available at stationery or craft supply stores), using a child's hand as your template. Write party details on decorative tag cards. Punch a hole in each card, loop string through the hole, and tie the card around one of the handprint's fingers to remind guests to come to the shower.

Handprint Invitations

🐣

Decorations

→ Decorate materials, tablecloths, and gift-wrap with handmade baby footprints. (See Baby Footprints Invitations for instructions.)

Baby Footprint Décor

🐣

→ Make a bouquet of rosebuds from baby socks for a centerpiece. Follow these instructions to make the sock rosebuds:

Thin baby socks with ruffles (one sock per rosebud)
Bouquet of artificial roses
Green floral tape

*Baby Sock
Rosebud Bouquet*

Tightly roll each sock from the toe to the heel to form a rosebud. Pull the sock cuff up and around the bud to secure. Cut off the buds from the artificial roses and insert a sock rosebud on each stem. Secure the sock rosebuds to the stems with green floral tape. Place the sock rosebuds in a vase and give the bouquet to the mom-to-be after the shower.

→ Wire a few sock rosebuds to a lightweight rattle along with ribbon bow to make a corsage for the mom-to-be. Use a diaper pin to attach the corsage to clothing.

Activities

→ Design a personalized baby book to store photos of baby and other mementoes. Buy a large scrapbook and leave room on the cover for baby's foot- and handprints. Provide plenty of stickers, rubber stamps, paint, markers, scissors, glue, and other scrapbooking supplies for guests to decorate the inside pages. Be sure to set up ample workspace before the party begins. Cover tabletops with old or vinyl tablecloths. Divide guests into work areas and assign each to decorate a page with a theme like the following:

Waiting for Baby	*Baby's Shower*
Baby's Birth	*Baby's Homecoming*
Baby's First Bath	*Baby's First Outing*
Baby's First Smile	*Baby's First Holiday*

Use an instant or digital camera to take a photo of each guest with the mom-to-be. Encourage guests to incorporate these photos into their scrapbooking designs.

→ Try this hands-on activity that's sure to leave guests tickled. Gift-wrap a small inexpensive gift item (for example, a votive candle, bath beads, or a sachet). Seat guests in a circle and give the mom-to-be the wrapped gift. Instruct guests that each time they hear the words *left* and *right* in the story about the Wright family (see page 126), they must pass the gift to the person in that direction. The guest holding the gift at the end of the story gets to unwrap it and take it home. (If your guest list is large, you may want to use more than one gift so everyone stays involved.)

→ The name of the game is Multitasking Mama. This is a relay race in which teammates each dash to a pile of baby socks while holding a baby doll in one hand and a cordless phone in the other. The first contestants for each team must match and fold the pairs of socks together—all while managing to hang on to the doll and phone. If a contestant drops the phone or the baby, she must start the task over. When the first contestants have matched and folded the socks, they hand the doll and phone to the next teammates, who must dash to the socks, unfold them, mix them up, then hand the doll and phone to the next teammates. This process continues until all the teammates have run the race. The team that completes these tasks first wins. For a smaller group, you may want to individually time each contestant and award a prize to the one who matches and folds the socks the quickest. Give the socks to the mom-to-be after the race.

Gifts

→ Invite guests to bring items that will protect or pamper baby's hands or feet, like mittens, warm baby socks, and baby nail clippers.

→ Give the mom-to-be everything she'll need to make a keepsake handprint of her future child. Tie ribbon around a bag of plaster of Paris and present it in a shallow decorative tin. Include the following poem typed in a child's handwriting font:

Wright Family Story

❦

Multitasking Mama

❦

Pampering Gifts

❦

Keepsake Handprint

Keepsake Handprint

Sometimes you get frustrated
Because I am so small
And always leave my handprints
On windows and on walls.
But time moves by too quickly,
And messes I have made
Including little handprints
Will surely start to fade.
So here's a special handprint
In order to recall
Just how my little hand looked
When I was oh-so small.

Spa Gift Certificate

→ Invite guests to contribute to a spa or salon gift certificate for the mom-to-be to have her feet pampered. After all, it's been some time since she's seen them!

Favors

→ Make paper cup booties for the guests. Follow these instructions to make each bootie:

Decorative-edged and standard scissors
7-ounce paper cup in pink, blue, or baby motif
Hole punch
16-inch ribbon or shoelace
Candies or mints

Paper Cup Booties

Use the decorative-edged scissors to cut about 1 inch off the top of the paper cup. To make the bootie's tongue, use the standard scissors to cut 2 slits about 2 inches apart, starting from the top of the cup to about 1 inch from the bottom. Push the tongue back and fold the 2 sides over it. Punch shoelace holes through all the layers. Lace the bootie with ribbon and tie the ribbon in a bow to secure the bootie's shape. Fill the bootie with candies or mints.

→ Stuff potpourri in baby socks with ruffles. Tie the socks closed with ribbon and attach to each sock a note card that features a note of thanks and the following poem:

> *Two things in life*
> *Are very sweet…*
> *Good friends like you*
> *And babies' feet!*

→ Make Pat-a-Cakes for the guests. Dip Oreo cookies in melted chocolate (see Oreo Rattles on page 89 for details). Once the chocolate has hardened, use frosting to pipe the letter *B* on each cookie top. Place each cookie in a small box along with a note card that features the Pat-a-Cake rhyme.

→ Make a batch of Pitter Patter, Pat-a-Cake Sugar Cookies (see the recipe below). Decorate clean, empty Chinese food containers with handmade baby footprints (see Baby Footprints Invitations on page 27). Fill the containers with the cookies and give as favors.

Food

Finger foods of all kinds would definitely be apropos at this shower. Try the following recipes in celebration of baby's feet:

→ Make Cheesy "Foot"balls. Flatten two nut-covered cheese balls with a rolling pin. Use a template (see instructions below) to cut baby's left foot from one cheese ball and baby's right foot from the other. Set the footprints, one footprint in front of the other, on a serving platter. Surround the footprints with a decorative ring of parsley. Add five sliced almonds to each footprint for toenails. Serve with crackers and bread.

→ Make Pitter Patter, Pat-a-Cake Sugar Cookies or Petit Fours. Use a hand- or foot-shaped cookie cutter to cut shapes from refrigerated sugar cookie dough (or use the recipe on page 117). If these cookie cutters prove hard to find, draw a handprint or footprint on heavy card stock and cut it out. Use it to cut the shapes from

Potpourri Baby Socks

Pat-a-Cakes

Pitter Patter,
Pat-a-Cake Cookies

Cheesy "Foot"balls

Sugar Cookies or
Petit Fours

the dough with a sharp knife. Flip the template to make the opposite hand or foot shape. Transfer the dough cutouts to baking sheets and bake the cookies according to the recipe's instructions. Use the recipe on page 116 to ice the cookies.

Or cut the same shapes from a jellyroll cake. Preheat your oven to 350°F. To make the cake, prepare an 18-ounce package of white cake mix according to package instructions and pour the batter into a 15-by-10-by-1-inch greased jellyroll pan. Bake the cake for 25 minutes. Cool the cake, then carefully remove it from the pan. Wrap the cake with plastic wrap and freeze it for 1 hour to make for easier cutting and fewer crumbs. Remove the plastic wrap and use the cookie cutter or template to cut hand or foot shapes from the cake. Use the recipe on page 116 to ice the tops and sides of the cakes. Outline the shape of each hand or foot with pink or blue icing.

→ Baby Bootie Cakes

18-ounce package white cake mix (plus ingredients called for on package)
Four 16-ounce cans white frosting (Use the recipe on page 115 to make your own.)
Toothpicks
Red or blue food coloring
Ribbon in a coordinating color

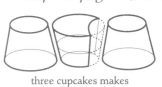

three cupcakes makes
two bootie cakes

Prepare and bake a batch of 24 cupcakes according to package instructions. Allow the cupcakes to cool, then remove the liners. Wrap 8 cupcakes with plastic wrap and put them in the freezer for 30 minutes to make for easier cutting and fewer crumbs. For each pair of Baby Bootie Cakes, you'll need 1 chilled cupcake and 2 room temperature cupcakes. Remove the plastic wrap from the chilled cupcake, then cut out a small semicircle, cutting down through the whole cupcake. Then slice the cupcake in half horizontally. Turn the other 2 cupcakes upside down and set a cupcake half against each upside down cupcake to make a bootie shape. Secure the cupcake pieces with toothpicks and cover the booties with white frosting. Tint ½ cup of frosting pink or blue. Place the tinted frosting in a pastry bag (or see page 116 to make your own pastry bag) and use it to pipe on frosting shoelaces on each bootie. Finish by adding a coordinating ribbon bow. This recipe makes 8 pairs of Baby Bootie Cakes.

→ Make tiny handprint and footprint chocolate dessert garnishes. See page 117 for instructions.

Baby Bootie Cakes

❦

Handprint or Footprint Garnishes

Baby 101

This shower is perfect for the first-time mom who needs to learn everything there is to know about having and caring for babies.

Invitations

→ For each invitation, write party details and the following poem on a blank note card.

She's new at this and nervous, too.
Our mom-to-be could use a clue.
So take this card designed for you.
And write down what a mom would do.

Baby Advice Invitations

On another note card, jot down a question about baby care. (For example, "How do you take care of a baby's umbilical cord?") Ask guests to write down their answers below the questions and bring the note cards to the shower. Punch a hole in a corner of each card and tie both cards to a baby paper doll with ribbon. Mail the invitations in large envelopes. Or tie the cards to small, inexpensive baby dolls and mail in padded envelopes or small boxes. At the shower, cut the questions from the responses and put them into separate bowls. To entertain guests throughout the shower, select questions and random responses. The garbled motherly advice will be hilarious.

Chalkboard Invitations

→ Write party details with a fine-tip permanent white marker on small chalkboards. Mail the invitations in padded envelopes.

Baby Anatomy Invitations

→ This invitation is a lesson in baby anatomy. To begin, find a cute photo of a baby. Make copies of the photo and glue a copy onto a large note card. Draw arrows pointing to its different body parts and make humorous notations about their functions. (For example, add an arrow to baby's bottom with a note that reads, "Diaper this end!")

Decorations

→ At the entrance, write "Welcome to Baby 101" on a child's chalkboard. Give it to the mom-to-be following the celebration.

→ For a table centerpiece, frame a collection of the mom-to-be's childhood school photos. Make special notations about degrees or awards she's earned. You may also place a collage of these photos in a large frame and use it as a serving tray for hors d'oeuvres.

→ Borrow a mortarboard (or make one from card stock) to adorn the mom-to-be. Add a tassel made from blue and pink embroidery floss. At the end of the party when the mom-to-be has passed Baby 101 and earned her degree in motherhood, move the tassel from the right to left side. If you like, complete the graduate look by having her wear a choir robe.

→ And finally, if you would really like to give the guest of honor a good belly laugh, invite the guests to dress up like pregnant women. A first-time mom-to-be may enjoy not feeling as though she's the only "big one" at the party. Award a prize to the guest with the best costume.

Activities

→ This icebreaker gives new meaning to "breaking your water." Pour water halfway in ice cube tray sections. When the water's frozen, place a tiny plastic baby in each section, fill the sections with water, and freeze again. Place the ice cubes in separate paper cups and give a cup to each guest upon arrival. Challenge the guests to "break their water" by melting the ice in any way you've deemed permissible. The first guest to free her baby from the ice and yell "My water broke!" wins a suitable prize, like a bath towel or colorful sarong to wrap around her waist. If tiny plastic babies prove hard to find, use Gummi bears instead.

Welcoming Chalkboard

❦

School Photo Centerpiece

❦

Mortarboard and Robe

❦

Expecting Guests

❦

My Water Broke!

→ Play Nightlife with Baby and give the mom-to-be a realistic picture of what nights with a newborn might soon look like through her tired eyes. Give players paper and markers. Blindfold the players or darken the room so they can't see their papers well. Ask them each to draw the following objects one at a time:

✔ A changing table
✔ A baby on the changing table
✔ A diaper on the baby
✔ A toy in the baby's hand
✔ A clock that reads 3:00 A.M.

Award a prize to the player who draws the most accurate picture.

→ Test the mom-to-be's baby knowledge with a pop quiz entitled Who Wants to Be a Mommy? (see page 128). To play, seat the mom-to-be on center stage. Pose one question at a time from the list along with possible answers from which she must choose a "final answer." She may also use three "lifelines" if needed: 1) She can use the 50-50 option in which half the choices will be eliminated, leaving her to choose the correct answer from the two that remain; 2) she may ask the guests to vote for the correct answer with a show of hands; 3) she can phone someone (for example, her mother or the dad-to-be) for help. Each of these options may be used only once. She may opt out at any time and still keep the prizes accumulated at each milestone. (Milestones are questions 5, 10, and 15.) When she passes each milestone, present her first with a container of baby wipes, then a package of newborn diapers, and finally a diaper bag—all things she'll need to be a mom!

Gifts

→ Invite guests to bring gifts that emphasize good mothering. For example, suggest bringing safety items like cabinet locks, outlet plug covers, or corner bumpers. Another suggestion is to bring gifts that will help mom and baby bond, like a storybook, baby carrier, or a how-to book on baby massage.

→ To ensure the baby gifts aren't quickly outgrown, in the invitations assign each guest to a different baby age and ask her to bring a developmental toy that corresponds. For example, a crib gym is a hit for a 3-month-old, while pull toys are much enjoyed by a one-year-old who's learning to walk.

→ A first-time mom is anxious about the whole labor and delivery process. Help her relax by giving her notes written by guests to read during a long labor and during her recovery. Buy pretty note cards and envelopes and hand a set to each guest upon arrival. Ask her to write the mom-to-be an encouraging note before leaving the shower. Stack the notes, tie with ribbon, and pack them with the gifts the mom-to-be receives.

Favors

→ Present to guests school supplies that can be put to good use around the home. For example, give rulers along with notes that read, "My thanks cannot be measured! Thanks for attending Baby 101 with my mommy! Love, Baby [baby's first or last name]."

→ Give each guest a gift certificate in a small amount (rolled and tied with ribbon to look like a diploma) to a bookstore, art store, or other educational store. Add a note of thanks and congratulations for passing Baby 101.

Food

→ Baby 101 Diplomas

1 cup ranch dressing	2 cups shredded mozzarella cheese
Ten 9-inch flour tortillas	3 cups shredded romaine lettuce
1 pound thinly sliced honey ham	2 large tomatoes, chopped
1 pound thinly sliced smoked turkey	20 slices bacon, cooked and crumbled

Gifts for Growing Baby

❧

Encouraging Notes

❧

School Supplies

❧

Gift Certificate Diplomas

❧

Baby 101 Diplomas

Spread the dressing onto each tortilla, leaving a ½-inch border all around. Layer the remaining ingredients onto each tortilla. Tightly roll the tortillas and wrap a ribbon bow around each one.

If you'd rather serve sweet-tasting diplomas, blend cream cheese with raspberry jam. Spread the mixture onto the tortillas. Roll the tortillas and secure them with strips cut from dried fruit rolls.

→ Serve Baby Cakes. Decorate cupcakes to resemble babies portraying a variety of emotions. Use an assortment of candies, cereal, frosting, and pacifiers. Serve the cupcakes on plates and set a card stock speech bubble next to each cupcake. Write the baby cakes' sentiments on the bubbles.

→ Bake a Baby Anatomy Cake. Use your favorite recipe, or the recipe on page 115, to bake a 13-by-9-inch cake. Allow the cake to cool, then carefully remove the cake from the pan. Wrap the cake with plastic wrap and freeze it for 1 hour to make for easier cutting and fewer crumbs. Cut out a large gingerbread man shape from a 13-by-9-inch piece of wax paper. Remove the plastic wrap from the cake, then lay the gingerbread man cutout on the cake and use a knife to cut around the shape. Transfer the cutout cake onto a large cake board that's covered with butcher paper. Decorate the cake with skin-toned frosting. Use pink or blue cake decorating sprinkles to add a diaper and a variety of candies for other facial features, and so on. When the cake is finished, draw arrows and write clever quips about baby's body parts with marker on the paper in appropriate places. This recipe makes 9 servings.

Noah's Ark

You'll have double the fun with this shower theme. It's terrific for twins, but works equally great for singles.

Invitations

→ Cut ark shapes from brown card stock. Decorate each ark with markers and animal stickers (two of each animal, of course). Or for a three-dimensional effect, glue a matching pair of animal crackers onto each ark and mail the invitations in padded envelopes.

Ark Invitations

→ Cut small matching pairs of animal shapes from card stock. On one animal in each pair, write, "A flood of joy is on the way for [mom-to-be's name], so let's have a Noah's Ark shower. Please bring a pair of anything for baby." On the other animals in the pairs, write the party details. Insert the animal pairs into pairs of baby socks, and tie the socks together with decorative ribbon. Mail the invitations in padded envelopes.

Animal Pairs Invitations

→ Write party details on raindrop shapes cut from card stock. Add these poetic lines if one baby is on the way:

> *Here's a party that's double fun.*
> *Let's celebrate this little one.*

If the shower is for multiples, use this poem:

> *They're coming two-by-two.*
> *Could be pink or could be blue!*

Raindrop Invitations

Buy matching pairs of small plastic animals from a dollar or discount store, and attach a pair to each raindrop with silver ribbon. Mail the invitations in padded envelopes.

Decorations

→ Cut large raindrop shapes from card stock and hang them from the ceiling with metallic silver ribbon. Use fabric paint to write the following sentiment on a child's umbrella: "Showers of Good Wishes to [mom-to-be's name] and Baby." Hang the umbrella above the seat where the mom-to-be will sit. To make a keepsake for the guest of honor, have each guest sign the umbrella before leaving the shower.

→ Stencil or rubber stamp matching pairs of animals onto a buffet tablecloth. Use wire to attach matching pairs of small plush animals into a floral centerpiece.

→ Use cardboard to turn your buffet table into Noah's Ark. Cut a large semicircle from a refrigerator box to form one side of the ark's hull. Use a slightly smaller box for the ark's cabin. Cut the short flaps from the cabin box and cut out windows in a side panel. Fold up the long flaps of the box until their edges meet and tape the edges in place to form the cabin's roof. Paint all of the cardboard pieces brown. Use a black marker to draw boards and wood grain on the painted cardboard and write "Noah's Ark" on the hull. To build the ark, move your buffet table against the wall and cover the top with brown fabric. Punch a hole in each end of the hull. Thread clear fishing line through the holes and tie the hull to the table legs. Place the ark's cabin on top of the table. Insert matching pairs of small plush animals through the windows so they can peek through. (You may want to first set small boxes inside the cabin box to prop the toys up.)

Activities

→ This activity is a great icebreaker. Buy as many matching pairs of small toy animals as half the number of expected guests. For example, if you're expecting ten guests, you'll need five pairs of animals. Give each guest one animal upon arrival. When all the guests have arrived, have them find their animal matches. When a guest finds her match, have the two ask each other fun, get-to-know-you questions, such as "What's your favorite pair of anything?" or "What's the most embarrassing thing that's ever happened to you?" (You may want to provide lists of questions.) After everyone has had a chance to ask and answer a few questions, have each pair use the information to introduce each other to the other guests.

Or instead of having guests look for their matches, ask them to keep their animals hidden and, on your mark, simultaneously make their animals' sounds to attract their matches. When two guests decide they're a match, the pair must trot, swim, fly—whatever it takes to stay in character—to "Noah" (you or the mom-to-be). There they'll see if they've correctly "mated" by revealing their toy animals to each other. This game is all the more fun if talking isn't allowed.

→ Have the guests decorate a menagerie of onesies for the baby using animal stencils and fabric paint.
Cardboard inserts to fit inside onesies
Wax paper
Plain onesies (prewashed and in a variety of sizes)
Tape
Animal stencils
Fabric paint
Paper plates
Stencil brushes

Cover each cardboard insert with wax paper and insert the cardboard into the onesies. Tape a stencil to each onesie. Squeeze fabric paint onto paper plates and set the brushes nearby. Ask guests to dab the paint inside the cutouts (rather than stroke the paint over the stencils) so the paint doesn't run under the edges of the stencils. Have the guests sign their names to their onesies.

Matching Animals Icebreaker

❦

Decorate the Onesies

→ Gather the guests in a circle. Have them take turns throwing a small plush animal to one another. Each guest who catches the animal must name one item that's needed for a baby's nursery. Or have the guest throwing the animal say an animal name and have the guest catching the animal say the baby name for that same animal. For example, if someone says "dog," the guest catching the animal must say "puppy." In either version of the game, no item can be said more than once. If a guest can't come up with a new item or the correct baby name, she's out of the game. The last guest in the game is the winner.

Gifts

→ Ask guests in the invitations each to bring a pair of something for baby (pair of shoes, pair of buddies like Bert and Ernie, or simply doubles of essentials like sleepers and diapers). Or ask them to bring gifts that will keep the little one dry, such as a child's umbrella, towels, or even diapers.

→ Make a towel cake that can serve as a gift for the mom-to-be and as a centerpiece for the gift or buffet table. For each layer of the cake, you'll need the following items:

Matching towel and washcloth set
Baby socks, bibs, and other baby garments (optional)
Several 1½-inch white pearl boutonniere pins
2½-by-36-inch decorative ribbon
Inexpensive toy animals
Several pairs of baby socks
Ribbon bows or streamers (optional)

Fold the long edges of the towel to meet in the center. Fold the washcloth and any baby garments lengthwise. Place them at equal intervals along the center of the towel. Fold the long edges of the towel to meet in the center again, covering the washcloth and garments. Roll the towel up starting with a short edge. Secure the rolled towel with the pins. Use pins to attach decorative ribbon to the rolled towel. Repeat this process using a smaller towel for each additional layer. Decorate the cake top with matching pairs of toy animals and flowers made from baby socks. (To make the sock flowers, scrunch the toes through the openings of the socks to form "petals.") Attach the animals and sock flowers with pins. If desired, finish with ribbon bows or streamers.

→ In the invitations, assign a different color of the rainbow to each guest. Ask guests to bring gifts that correspond to their assigned colors.

Favors

→ Wrap animal crackers in cellophane and ribbon. Cut ark-shaped tags from brown card stock, write your thanks on each tag, and attach one to each bundle of animal crackers.

→ Let guests each choose a matching pair of animal cookie pops. To make the cookies, roll out sugar cookie dough on a floured surface. (Use the sugar cookie recipe on page 117 or use refrigerated cookie dough.) Use animal-shaped cookie cutters to cut out pairs of each animal. Before placing the animal cutouts on the baking sheet, insert a 4-inch lollipop stick into the side of each cutout at the bottom of the animal. (You can find lollipop sticks in the baking supplies section of a grocery or discount store.) Bake the cookies, then decorate them as desired. Place a floral foam brick in a decorative window box and stick the animal cookie pops into the foam. Conceal the foam with pastel-colored paper shreds.

→ Give guests each a matching pair of something, like candles or items that feature animals.

Towel Cake

Rainbow Color Gifts

Animal Cracker Bundles

Animal Cookie Pops

Favor Pairs

Food

→ Prepare matching pairs of animal-shaped sandwiches. Place chicken salad or other sandwich material between two slices of dense bread. Cover the sandwiches and refrigerate them to make for easier cutting. Press a sharp animal-shaped cookie cutter in the center of each sandwich.

→ Garnish favorite desserts with filigree chocolate animal shapes. To make the chocolate animals, use animal-shaped cookie cutters or animals cut from coloring books as guides and follow the instructions on page 117.

→ Noah's Ark Cake

Two 10.75-ounce frozen pound cakes
Two 13-by-9-inch cakes, cooled (Prepare the cakes from packaged mixes or double the recipe on page 115.)
Four 16-ounce cans chocolate frosting
Iced animal crackers or pairs of small toy animals
Blue-tinted coconut (optional)

Thaw the pound cakes. Carefully remove the sheet cakes from the pans, then wrap each in plastic wrap. Freeze the sheet cakes for 1 hour to make for easier cutting and fewer crumbs. Remove the plastic wrap, then level the tops of the sheet cakes. Place one sheet cake on a cake board and frost its top. Place the other sheet cake on top of the first. Carve away the corners of the sheet cakes as illustrated. Set one pound cake on the center of the sheet cakes and frost its top. Place the other pound cake on top of the first. Cut away the sides of the top pound cake as illustrated to make a roof. Secure the cake structure with toothpicks if necessary before frosting it entirely. Decorate the ark with animal crackers or pairs of small toy animals. If desired, cover exposed cake board with blue-tinted coconut. (To tint the coconut, place it in a plastic bag, then add equal drops of blue food coloring and water. Seal the bag and shake the contents until the desired color is achieved.) This recipe makes 30 servings.

→ Rainbow Punch

2 quarts sweetened blueberry Kool-Aid
46-ounce can pineapple juice
½ gallon rainbow sherbet
1-liter bottle ginger ale

Mix the first 2 ingredients together in a large pitcher and refrigerate the liquid until it's chilled. To serve, pour the chilled liquid into a punch bowl and float sherbet scoops in the liquid. Top with ginger ale. Browse a Christian bookstore or gift store to find a toy ark to float in the bowl. Add a drink umbrella to each glass. This recipe makes fifty 4-ounce servings.

TEDDY BEAR PICNIC

Base your celebration around these classic childhood companions, and your guests are certain to have a "beary" good time.

Invitations

→ Scent sandpaper by rubbing cinnamon sticks on the sheets. Using a teddy-bear-shaped cookie cutter as a template, cut teddy bear shapes from the scented sandpaper. Glue a pink or blue ribbon bow onto each bear's neck and use a black marker to add facial features. Glue each bear onto the front of a folded card stock card and write party details inside.

→ Draw a teddy bear head shape on card stock and cut the shape out. Use the template to cut heads from brown furry fabric. Write party details on the backs of decorative note cards, and glue the heads onto the fronts. Glue a pair of googly eyes and a black felt nose and mouth onto each head. Glue a blue- or pink-checked ribbon bow tie below each head.

→ Buy inexpensive small plush bears and tie a diaper made from a triangular piece of blue or pink fabric on each bear. Write party details on decorative tags, attach a tag to each bear, and mail the bears in small boxes punched with "air holes." Add labels to the boxes that read, "Shhh…Baby Bear Sleeping!" or "Handle with Care—There's a Bear Inside!"

Decorations

→ If weather permits, hold the party outdoors. Spread large quilts on the ground for guests to sit on. (Provide a decorated lawn chair for the guest of honor, as getting up from the ground may be challenging for her.) Tie balloon bouquets to teddy bears and place the bears inside picnic baskets. Set a basket on the center of each quilt. Instead of using a traditional red-and-white-checked tablecloth on the buffet table, create a pink- or blue-checked

Scented Teddy Bear Invitations

Teddy Head Invitations

Bear-in-a-Box Invitations

Teddy Bear Picnic Setting

tablecloth. Buy an inexpensive white tablecloth, pink or blue fabric paint, and a square sponge, and stamp a checked design on the tablecloth. Remember that an outdoor party requires a few necessities to make things "bearable" including insect repellent and sunscreen. If necessary, a big piece of green artificial turf will allow you to bring the outdoors in and leave the bugs behind.

→ Dress assorted bears in diapers, decorated onesies, or pajamas. Set them around the party area. Give all the bears to the mom-to-be after the party.

→ Make bear balloons to decorate the party area.

Pink or blue balloons
Helium tank (optional)
Black permanent marker
Scissors
Pink or blue construction paper
Decorative ribbon
Curling ribbon
Double-sided tape

Inflate the balloons with helium. Draw a bear face on each balloon. Cut a pair of ears from the construction paper and stick them onto the balloon with double-sided tape. Add a decorative ribbon bow tie at the bottom of the balloon, and tie the balloon to curling ribbon cut to the desired length. Anchor the balloons to jars of honey.

Activities

→ Fill a clear baby bottle with many yellow jellybeans and some black ones. Shake the bottle so a few black "honeybees" can be seen. Challenge guests to guess how many honeybees are in the hive. The guest who guesses closest to the correct number wins a prize.

Keepsake Photo Album

Tear Bears

*The Bear Went
Over the Mountain*

→ Make a keepsake photo album of the shower for the mom-to-be. Buy a large blank journal and assign each guest a page to decorate with bear-related stickers, stamps, and stencils. Remind the guests to leave room on each page for photos. Using a digital or instant camera, take photos throughout the party. Glue the photos into the album, making sure to leave a few pages blank so photos of the baby can be added later. Title the photo album "A 'Beary' Good Time Was Had By All."

→ Divide the guests into teams of two. Have teammates sit facing each other with their knees touching. Give each duo a sheet of brown construction paper and instruct them to use only their left hands to tear a bear shape from the paper. Tell them that laughing is permitted, but talking during play is not allowed. Award prizes for the best tear bears.

→ Challenge guests to play The Bear Went Over the Mountain. After singing the first stanza of the song as a group, the first player says a baby-related item that the bear saw on the other side of the mountain. Each subsequent player must list the stated items in the correct order, plus add a new item to the list. Here are the song lyrics. Sing them to the tune of "For He's a Jolly Good Fellow."

> *The bear went over the mountain,*
> *The bear went over the mountain,*
> *The bear went over the mountain,*
> *To see what he could see.*

Gifts

↪ Send guests on a bear hunt. In the invitations, assign each guest a bear featured in a song or book and ask her to bring a gift for baby that corresponds. Consider the following list:

Bear in the Big Blue House
The Berenstain Bears
Corduroy
Little Bear
Paddington Bear
Goldilocks and the Three Bears
Winnie-the-Pooh

Or assign a guest a kind of bear, like a grizzly or panda, and ask her to bring a gift that corresponds.

↪ Invite guests to bring the "bare" necessities for baby, such as tubes of diaper rash cream, baby cereal, or wet wipes. Inspire the mom-to-be to bare her body after the baby's born: give her a wearable teddy.

↪ For a warm fuzzy feeling, invite everyone to bring a small plush bear to donate to your local children's hospital or women's shelter. The donated bears will provide comfort to people in need. You may choose to make the collective donation anonymously or attach to each bear a gift tag that reads, "This bear hug has been donated to you in celebration of Baby [baby's first or last name]."

Favors

↪ Wrap Gummi bears or teddy-bear-shaped crackers in cellophane squares and tie the bundles with ribbon. Attach to each bundle a note card that reads, "Thank you 'beary' much for coming!"

↪ Send guests home with goodies to help them hibernate, like relaxing bath oils, tea, eye masks, or beeswax candles.

Bear Hunt Gifts

❦

Bare Necessities

❦

Bear Donation

❦

Bear Bundles

❦

Hibernation Gifts

Food

Pack individual picnic lunches in small baskets that can double as party favors. Include any of the following delicious recipes.

→ "Beary" Good Trail Mix

4 cups Honey Nut Cheerios cereal
4 cups Teddy Grahams snacks
3 cups honey-roasted peanuts
1 cup raisins
1 cup pink or blue M&M's (optional)

Mix all the ingredients in a large bowl. Cover the mix until serving. This recipe makes twenty ⅔-cup servings.

→ Bear Buns

Three 1-pound frozen bread dough loaves
1 egg
54 raisins

Thaw the loaves in the refrigerator overnight. Divide each loaf into 6 equal portions. From each portion, roll 1 large ball and 3 small ones. On a lightly greased baking sheet, flatten each large ball to make the bear's face. Place 2 small balls at the top for ears. Press 1 small ball onto the face for the bear's nose. Top the nose with a raisin and add raisin eyes. Cover the bears with plastic wrap, then set them aside for a couple of hours until the dough has doubled in size. Preheat your oven to 350°F. Whisk the egg in a small bowl, then brush the egg onto the bears. Bake the bears for 15 minutes or until golden brown. Serve them whole or sliced with your favorite sandwich materials.

→ Serve Bear Cookies. Prepare your favorite chocolate chip cookie dough recipe, but leave out the chips. For each bear's face, place one large ball of cookie dough onto a greased baking sheet and flatten it. Add two small balls of dough at top to form the bear's ears. When the cookies are golden brown, remove them from

"Beary" Good Trail Mix

🐻

Bear Buns

🐻

Bear Cookies

the oven and press a chocolate kiss nose and two brown mini-M&M eyes on each bear. Allow the cookies to cool before serving.

→ Make a Teddy Bear Cake. Bake two 9-inch round cakes and seven cupcakes. (Prepare the cakes from packaged mixes or make 1½ batches of the recipe on page 115.) Set the round cakes side by side on a cake board. Place six of the cupcakes in place next to the round cakes to make the bear's ears, arms, and legs. Cover the bear cake with pink or blue frosting. Frost the last cupcake and place it upside down in the center of the bear's face. Use gum-drops, pastel-colored M&M's, and licorice to add facial features, a belly-button, and a diaper. This recipe makes 18 servings.

Teddy Bear Cake

→ Berry Honey Tea

16-ounce package frozen whole strawberries, thawed
⅔ cup honey
12-ounce can frozen orange juice concentrate, partially thawed
4 cups brewed green tea, cooled
Fresh strawberries (optional)

Berry Honey Tea

Mix the first 3 ingredients in a blender until smooth. Add the mixture to the tea and stir until blended. Serve the drink over ice and garnish with fresh strawberries, if desired. This recipe makes 8 servings.

Bottles, Bibs, & Blankies

Celebrate the arrival of a one-of-a-kind baby by featuring these quintessential baby items in your shower.

Invitations

→ Send baby bottle invitations. Write party details on note cards that include the caption, "We can't keep it bottled up any longer. We're having a baby shower for [mom-to-be's name]." Encourage guests to fill the bottles with coupons for baby products and bring the bottles to the shower. (Award a prize to the guest who collects the most valuable savings.) Place the invitations in plastic baby bottles, and secure the bottle tops with clear packing tape. The bottles will act as mailing tubes. Write the guests' addresses on label stickers, and stick a label on each bottle. Take the bottles to your post office to buy postage.

→ Make paper plate bib invitations. For each invitation, cut out a neckline from a small pastel-colored paper plate to make a bib. Punch a hole in each top corner of the bib and thread decorative ribbon through each hole. Write party details on the bib.

→ Include a small square piece of plain colored fabric with each invitation. Write these instructions on separate small card stock squares: "Help make a great gift for baby. Decorate the square however you like and bring it to the shower." Use a diaper pin to attach the instructions to each fabric square. After the shower, sew the squares together to make a keepsake baby quilt that'll warm baby's toes and mom's heart.

Baby Bottle Invitations

Paper Plate
Bib Invitations

Quilt Square Invitations

Decorations

➜ Place flower bouquets in baby bottles filled with sand. For a special touch, use silk flowers and glue a bottle nipple onto each flower's center. Or use the bottles as candleholders. Fill the bottles with colored sand and insert taper candles in the sand. (Candles that don't drip wax work best.) Fit glass candle rings around the candles, and wrap ribbon around the bottle tops below the candle rings. Remember to never leave burning candles unattended.

➜ Transform baby blankets into babies and prop them around the party area. Follow these instructions to make each blanket baby:

30-by-40-inch receiving blanket (solid color)
5 sheets tissue paper
Infant hat and booties
Pacifier
Large sturdy rubber band
Tape measure
Pink and blue embroidery floss
Needle
Scissors

Lay the blanket flat. Set 2 sheets of tissue paper completely on the blanket, aligning each sheet along a short side of the blanket. (The tissue paper will give the blanket baby support.) Tightly roll each short side of the blanket to the center, leaving enough room between the 2 rolls to place a ball of tissue paper made from the remaining 3 sheets. Place the tissue paper ball about 10 inches from one of the blanket's unrolled edges and fold that same edge over the tissue ball. Secure the rubber band

Blanket Babies

below the ball to form the baby's head and arms. Fit the infant hat on the head. Make the baby's eyes, nose, and mouth by backstitching the embroidery floss in place. Sit the baby up and slip the booties on the baby's feet and sew the pacifier to baby's hands. Attach to each blanket baby a gift tag card that reads:

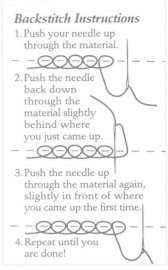

Backstitch Instructions
1. Push your needle up through the material.
2. Push the needle back down through the material slightly behind where you just came up.
3. Push the needle up through the material again, slightly in front of where you came up the first time.
4. Repeat until you are done!

> *With a scissors you can snip*
> *My eyes and mouth and nose.*
> *And you will have a blanket*
> *To warm dear baby's toes.*

Present the blanket babies to the mom-to-be following the festivities.

→ Substitute baby blankets for tablecloths. Use pacifiers as napkin rings. Serve drinks from baby bottles with straws. Wash the bottles following the shower and pack up all the baby items used for decorations for mom-to-be to take home.

Bottles & Blankies Décor

→ Fill the room with giant balloon pacifiers. Follow these instructions to make each pacifier:

Large pink or blue round balloon
Pink or blue twistable balloon with inflating pump
Sturdy white paper plate
Ice pick

Balloon Pacifiers

Use the pump to inflate the twistable balloon until it's almost full. Tie off the balloon. Bring the ends of balloon together and twist them together to form a pacifier handle. Use the ice pick to punch a hole in the center of a paper plate. Inflate the round balloon and tie it off. Set the round balloon on the plate and poke the knot through the hole. Tie the ends of the pacifier handle to the knot to make a balloon pacifier.

Activities

→ Buy a child's art easel and challenge guests to a few rounds of Baby Doodles. To play, photocopy the list on page 130 and cut it into individual slips of paper. Place the slips in the pouch of a baby bib and let the fun begin. Divide the guests into two teams. Have one player from Team 1 draw a slip and illustrate the item on the easel. The player may not talk or write letters and numbers as she illustrates her Baby Doodle. Her teammates must guess what she's drawing within an allotted time. If her teammates correctly identify the doodle, the team earns a point and a new member of the team draws a slip to illustrate. If Team 1 doesn't guess correctly, then Team 2 may make one guess. If Team 2 guesses correctly, it earns two points and one of its members takes to the drawing board. Set a time limit for the game, and award prizes to the highest scoring team when the game is called. Give the easel to the mom-to-be for the baby's future playroom.

→ Play Baby Bottle Bull's-Eye. For each player, cut a baby's face from card stock and cut out the mouth so it's wide enough to snugly fit around the rim of an empty baby food jar. Fit the baby face onto the jar. Fill plastic baby bottles with water tinted with food coloring and give a bottle to each player. (You may want to protect your floor in the game area with a plastic tablecloth.) Have players stand above their jars and, at your mark, begin squeezing water from the bottles into the babies' mouths. The player who squeezes the most water into her baby's mouth in the allotted time wins the race. With a large group, a relay race between teams may work best.

→ Fill a basket with bottles, bibs, blankies, and other baby essentials. Have the mom-to-be walk around the room holding the basket so each guest can quickly view the items. Once the mom-to-be has left the room, provide pencils and paper and ask guests to write down what they saw in the basket. Award

Baby Doodles

❦

Baby Bottle Bull's-Eye

❦

What's in the Basket?

a prize to the guest who recalls the most items. For a twist on this game, instead of asking guests to recall the items in the basket, ask them to answer questions about the mom-to-be's appearance (for example, "What's the color of her shirt?" "Is she wearing earrings?" and so on). When you've asked all the questions, have the mom-to-be return and award a prize to the guest who's answered the most questions correctly.

Gifts

→ Invite guests to house their gifts in bottles, or wrap them in bibs or blankies, and the packaging will be as useful as the gifts.

→ Make a bandana bib for baby.
Bandana and washcloth in coordinating colors
Matching thread
Scissors
Needle or sewing machine
Pins

Cut the bandana in half diagonally. Hem the cut edge of one half to prevent fraying. Lay the washcloth flat. Lay the bandana on the washcloth so its squared corner points toward you and the sides leading to this corner intersect with the washcloth's top corners. Pin the bandana to the washcloth and sew along the washcloth's top edge The ends of the bandana can be tied around baby's neck.

→ Folklore predicts that when the guest of honor opens the seventh gift, the person who gave that gift will be the next to have a baby. Surprise that gift-giver with a necklace made of strung-on pacifiers at the appropriate time.

→ For gift-opening fun, make a large bib from poster board. Punch two holes at the top of the bib and string ribbon through the holes. Tie the bib around the mom-to-be's neck when it's time to open gifts. Stick the gift bows onto the bib as the packages are opened. Keep your camera handy!

Favors

→ Make pacifier mints.

2 white Life Saver mints per favor
1 pink or blue oval-shaped candy per favor
1 teaspoon icing per favor (Use the recipe on page 116 to make your own.)

For each favor, lay one mint flat on a baking sheet. Stand the other mint on its side in the center of the first mint and use icing to attach them together. Allow the icing to harden. Use more icing to attach an oval-shaped candy to the other side of the first mint. When the icing has hardened, place each candy pacifier in a small clear cellophane bag and seal the bag with stickers in a baby motif.

→ Give each guest a baby bottle filled with lotion or bath crystals. (See page 75 to make your own bath crystals.) Add a decorative ribbon and a personalized label to each bottle.

Food

→ Stencil baby bottles and bibs on a wooden salad bowl. Fill the bowl with your favorite green salad. Serve salad dressings in baby bottles. Present the salad bowl to the mom-to-be following the shower.

Gift-Opening Bow Bib

❧

Pacifier Mints

❧

Baby Bottle Lotion or Bath Crystals

❧

Baby Bottle & Bib Salad

→ Baby Bottle Cake

Cake:
   1 cup flour
   1¼ teaspoons baking powder
   ½ teaspoon salt
   5 egg whites
   ⅓ cup sugar
   3 egg yolks
   1 teaspoon vanilla extract
   ⅓ cup sugar
   Powdered sugar
Filling:
   ½ cup water
   ½ cup sugar
   3 tablespoons lemon
      juice
   2 tablespoons corn starch
   1 teaspoon grated lemon peel
   2 drops yellow food coloring
Decorations:
   3 cups white frosting
   Yellow and pink or blue food coloring
   Yellow sugar sprinkles
   Large yellow gumdrop
   Toothpick

Baby Bottle Cake

Preheat your oven to 375°F. Grease a 15-by-10-by-1-inch jelly-roll pan and a 6-ounce custard cup. Line the jellyroll pan with wax paper and spray cooking spray on the wax paper. In a small bowl, combine the flour, baking powder, and salt. In another small bowl, beat the egg whites on high until foamy, then slowly beat in ⅓ cup sugar until the mixture makes stiff peaks. In a large bowl, beat the egg yolks, vanilla, and ⅓ cup sugar on high for 5 minutes. Fold the flour mixture and the egg white mixture into the egg yolk mixture. Pour ⅓ cup of batter into the custard cup. Pour the remaining batter into the jellyroll pan, spreading the batter evenly and making sure it reaches all corners of the pan. Bake both cakes for 8 minutes or until the cake tops spring back when touched. Let the custard cup cake stand for 10 minutes before transferring it to a wire rack to cool. Immediately turn the jellyroll cake onto a clean dishtowel sprinkled with powdered sugar. Remove the pan and gently peel the wax paper off the cake. Starting with one of the short sides, roll the cake up in the towel and allow it to cool. While the rolled cake cools, use a whisk to mix all the filling ingredients in a small saucepan. Bring the mixture to a boil over medium heat, stirring constantly. Boil for 1 minute. Remove the pan from the heat. Unroll the cooled cake and spread the filling all over the top of it. Roll up the cake again and place it seam side down on a cake board. Frost the cake with white frosting. Mix ⅓ cup of white frosting with 2 drops of yellow food coloring and use it to frost the cooled custard cup cake, then cover this cake with yellow sugar sprinkles. Place the custard cup cake so its flat side sticks to one end of the rolled cake. Stick the yellow gumdrop onto one end of the toothpick and insert the other end into the top of the custard cup cake to form the tip of bottle's nipple. Tint the remaining frosting pink or blue and fill a pastry bag with it. (See page 116 to make your own pastry bag.) Use the pink or blue frosting to decorate the rolled cake like a bottle, complete with measurement markings. This recipe makes 8 servings.

→ If you're short on time, buy a bundt cake from your local bakery and place it on a cake plate. Drizzle smooth icing (use the recipe on page 116 to make your own) tinted pink or blue over the cake. Pour candy into a decorated baby bottle and set the bottle into the cake's center. Or add chocolate garnishes in baby-related designs to frosted cupcakes. See page 117 for details.

Baby Bottle Cake

❤

Baby Bottle Bundt Cake

It's Potty Time!

The fun you'll have at this hilarious nontraditional shower won't be an "accident"!

Invitations

→ Buy paper dolls or make your own from card stock. Cut diapers from pink or blue paper to fold around each doll. Write "It's Potty Time!" on the outside front of each diaper and write the party details on the inside. Pin the diapers on the dolls with small safety pins.

→ Write party details on tag cards and attach each card to a large diaper pin. Add a headline that reads, "It's Potty Time!"

→ Fold small felt pieces or decorative paper into diaper shapes. Secure each diaper with a diaper pin. Write party details on small note cards. Include a few diaper-related terms in the copy; for example: "Everyone Luvs a baby shower, especially one that Pampers [mom-to-be's name] with Huggies and much more!" Insert a card into each diaper.

Decorations

→ Around the party area, display balloon bouquets anchored to diaper-related products, like tubes of diaper rash cream or containers of diaper wipes. Or tie the balloons to plush animals wearing diapers.

→ Drape toilet-paper streamers around the party area.

→ Display a unique diaper wreath. If you like, use the diaper wreath to present a gift certificate for the mom-to-be. Simply tie the certificate to the wreath as a trimming.

Paper Doll Invitations

Diaper Pin Invitations

Diaper Invitations

Diaper Décor

Toilet Paper Streamers

Diaper Wreath

12 size-3 diapers
12-inch wreath form
Curling ribbon
Scissors
Inexpensive baby items (rattles, socks, small toys, and so on)
Decorative bow

Wrap the diapers around the wreath so the tabs face outward. Wrap curling ribbon tightly around each diaper just below the tabs. Fan out the edges of each diaper for a fuller look. Use the ribbon to tie on the baby items and add a decorative bow.

Activities

→ Challenge guests to a game of Pin the Diaper on the Baby. Have the players pair up and give each pair a baby doll, a cloth diaper, and two diaper pins. Instruct each player to keep one hand behind her back. Each pair must work together to diaper its baby doll. The first pair to secure their baby's diaper wins prizes.

→ Play the No-No Game. Make certain baby-related words off-limits. Give each guest a supply of diaper pins and list of taboo words upon arrival. Throughout the shower, guests must try to catch other guests saying the taboo words. If a guest catches an offender saying a taboo word, the offender must give that guest a diaper pin. The guest with the most pins at the end of the party wins a prize.

→ Set decorum aside for a hilarious game of Name That Poo. Buy ten different chocolate candy bars and melt them separately in microwave-safe bowls. Spoon the melted candy bars separately into numbered diapers. Give players paper and pencils and have them number their papers from 1 to 10. Players must closely examine the contents of each diaper and write the name of the candy bar next to the corresponding number. Award a set of the candy bars to the player who correctly identifies the most "poo."

Diaper Wreath

❦

Pin the Diaper on the Baby

❦

No-No Game

❦

Name That Poo

→ Stage a swaddling contest. Divide the players into small teams. Give each team two rolls of toilet paper and have each team choose a teammate to swaddle. At your mark, teams must race to wrap their chosen teammates in toilet paper from the neck down. The team to first swaddle its teammate using all the toilet paper wins prizes.

Gifts

→ Make decorative diapers or burp pads from inexpensive cloth diapers. Follow these instructions to make each one:

Thick cloth diaper
2 lengths grosgrain ribbon, each slightly
  longer than length of diaper
White thread
Scissors
Needle or sewing machine

Place one ribbon lengthwise over the left seam of the diaper, or about 4 inches from the diaper's outside left edge. To prevent fraying, fold under the top and bottom of the ribbon so they're flush with the diaper's edges. Sew all sides of the ribbon to the diaper using small stitches. Repeat this process with the other ribbon on the diaper's right side.

→ Include a decorative sheet of paper with each invitation and ask guests to jot down on the paper a toilet-training tip and bring the paper to the party. Gather the papers upon the guests' arrival, stack them, and punch holes along the left side. Loop ribbon through each hole and tie them to form a booklet. The mom-to-be will treasure this advice in a couple of years.

→ Invite guests each to bring a package of diapers. Encourage them to bring diapers in any size except newborn so the baby's bottom will be covered for many months. Or invite guests each to bring a diaper-related coupon. Put the coupons in an empty diaper wipe container to present to the mom-to-be.

Favors

→ Buy or make toiletries for the guests. Here's how to make handmade soaps with buried treasures:

Soap molds
Baby oil
Knife
Glycerin soap (available by the block at craft stores)
Glass measuring cup
Soap fragrance or dye (optional)
Rubbing alcohol in spray bottle
*Trinkets (plastic diaper pins, baby bracelets, flowers, and other
    items that can withstand water and moderate heat)*
Colorful plastic wrap
Sticker labels and pen

Lightly coat the soap molds with baby oil. Cut the glycerin block at its perforations or into 1-inch chunks and place them in the measuring cup. Melt the glycerin according to the manufacturer's instructions. Add fragrance or dye if you like. Pour the melted glycerin into the soap molds. Spray the glycerin with rubbing alcohol to minimize bubbles. Insert a trinket face down into each mold. If necessary, use a toothpick to hold the trinket in place until the glycerin starts to set. Once the bars are hard, pop the soap from the molds and tightly wrap each in colorful plastic wrap. Where the plastic wrap edges meet, stick a label that reads, "From [mom-to-be's name]'s shower to your shower!"

Diaper Treats

→ Give guests each a diaper full of treats. Buy inexpensive wash-cloths from a discount store. Cut each washcloth in half diagonally to form two triangles. Wrap Hershey's Hugs and Kisses chocolates in cellophane and ribbon, and place a bundle on each triangle. Fold the triangles like diapers around the bundles and secure with diaper pins that have small decorative beads threaded on them. Attach to each diaper a tag card that reads, "Hugs & Kisses from Baby! Thanks for coming to my 'potty'!"

Food

Diaper Sandwiches

→ Diaper Sandwiches

8-ounce package cream cheese, softened
10-ounce can of chicken
Dash of pepper
Dash of garlic salt
Two 8-ounce packages refrigerated crescent rolls
16 small decorative diaper pins

Preheat your oven to 375°F. Use a fork to mix the cream cheese with the chicken. Add the pepper and garlic salt to the mixture. Unroll the dough triangles on a baking sheet and spoon 1 tablespoon of the mixture onto each triangle. Fold the triangles to look like diapers and bake the diapers for 8 minutes or until they're golden brown. Pin a diaper pin in place on each diaper. This recipe makes 16 diaper sandwiches.

*Dirty Diaper
Sheet Cake*

→ Dirty Diaper Sheet Cake

13-by-9-inch white cake, cooled (Prepare the cake from a packaged
*   mix or use the recipe on page 115.)*
16-ounce can white frosting (Use the recipe on page 115 to make
*   your own.)*
Chocolate candy kiss
2 large decorative diaper pins

Carefully remove the cake from the pan and wrap it in plastic wrap. Freeze the cake for 1 hour to make for easier cutting and fewer crumbs. Remove the plastic wrap. Cut the cake corners to make a diaper shape and place the diaper cake on a cake board. Press a chocolate candy kiss into the cake near the bottom. Frost the cake top, making sure to cover the chocolate kiss. Add the diapers pins in place. When serving the cake, award a small prize to the guest who finds the "dirty diaper surprise" in her piece. This recipe makes 12 servings.

→ Serve Diapered Baby Cookies. Use a gingerbread man cookie cutter to cut shapes from sugar cookie dough. (Use refrigerated dough or use the recipe on page 117.) Transfer the shapes to a baking sheet and bake them according to the recipe's instructions. When the cookies are cool, add a diaper made from pink or blue frosting to each one. Pipe on frosting bellybuttons and facial features from a pastry bag (or see page 116 to make your own pastry bag).

→ Potty Punch

Two 3-ounce packages pineapple gelatin
¾ cup sugar
2 cups boiling water
46-ounce can pineapple juice
6 cups cold water
2-liter bottle ginger ale, chilled

Stir the gelatin and sugar into the boiling water until dissolved. Pour the mixture into a gallon container. Add the pineapple juice and cold water. Shake the mixture to blend. Freeze the punch and remove it from the freezer several hours before the party so it can begin to thaw. Pour the punch into a new baby potty seat and add ginger ale just before serving. Send the "punch bowl" home with the mom-to-be after the party. This recipe makes thirty 4-ounce servings.

Dirty Diaper Sheet Cake

❦

Diapered Baby Cookies

❦

Potty Punch

ABC

Throwing this alphabet party can be as easy as ABC!

Invitations

→ Write party details on index cards decorated with alphabet stickers. Enclose a magnetic alphabet letter with each invitation so guests can post the invitations on their refrigerators as reminders.

→ Buy an inexpensive set of alphabet blocks. Write party details on sticker labels cut to fit on the blocks' side panels. Mail the blocks in small boxes or hand-deliver them.

→ Write party details on the inside covers of small, inexpensive alphabet books. Tie ribbon around each book and mail them in padded envelopes.

Decorations

→ Visit a teaching supply store to find loads of inexpensive items to decorate the party area to look like a grade-school classroom.

→ For table centerpieces, fold index cards in half so the short edges meet, and stencil a different letter on each card. Stand the cards up, and next to each one display baby items that begin with the same letter as the card. For example, place rattles next to the card featuring the letter *R.* Give the mom-to-be all of the baby items after the party.

→ Adorn the buffet table with gigantic alphabet blocks. To make each block, wrap a large sturdy box in plain, light-colored gift-wrap and stencil a letter of the alphabet on each panel. (Or use your computer to print clipart alphabet designs and glue one onto each panel.) If you like, instead use a staple gun to secure felt around the boxes, and glue on felt letter cutouts in a contrasting color. As a focal point, you may want to spell the words *baby [baby's last name]* with small toy blocks.

→ Make baby bracelet place cards. At a craft store, buy alphabet beads to spell each guest's name. Punch two holes in the front side of a folded place card. (You can make your own place card from folded card stock.) Spell out a guest's name with beads and string the beads in order onto thin jewelry wire. Snip the wire, leaving a couple of inches on either side of the beads. Insert the wire ends through the holes. Coil the wire at both ends.

Baby Bracelet Place Cards

Activities

→ Gather guests for a game of Parent Speak. This game highlights classic parenting phrases that have stood the test of time. Divide the guests into two teams and seat the teams around a large pad of paper. On the paper write a series of blanks to represent the letters of a parenting phrase (see page 131 for phrase suggestions). Have the first team pick a letter. If the letter appears in the phrase, write it in. The team may make one guess to name the phrase. If it guesses incorrectly or if the letter doesn't appear in the phrase, it's the other team's turn to pick a letter. The team that identifies the most phrases wins prizes.

Parent Speak

→ Design a photo alphabet book for baby. Give each guest an 8½-by-11-inch sheet of card stock in a pretty color and a variety of scrapbooking supplies (markers, stickers, and other embellishments). Assign each guest a letter, and ask the guests to decorate their sheets to feature their letters. Remind them to leave room on the sheets for photos. Put the sheets in plastic page protectors and put the page protectors in a decorative binder. Suggest that the mom-to-be fill the album with photos of baby that somehow relate to the corresponding letters. For example, the *B* page could show baby in the bath.

Photo Alphabet Book

Photo Alphabet Blocks

Alphabet Letter Gifts

Mother's Bracelet

Personalized Name Gifts

Rubber Stamp Favors

.

Trinkets by the Letter

→ Make a set of photo blocks for baby. Before the shower, ask the mom-to-be for copies of photos of family members (or ask to borrow the photos so you can make copies). Buy several plain square wood blocks and smooth rough edges with sandpaper. Paint the blocks with nontoxic paint in vibrant colors. At the shower, have guests trim the photos and decoupage them to the sides of the blocks. Have guests paint the first letter of the subject in the photo. For example, a block featuring a photo of grandma will include the letter G. These darling blocks will not only help baby learn the alphabet, but also family members' names.

Gifts

→ In the invitations, assign a different letter to each guest and ask her to bring a gift that corresponds.

→ Invite guests to contribute funds to buy a gift certificate for a mother's bracelet or necklace that features baby's name and birth date.

→ Plan to have the shower take place after the baby is born so guests can bring gifts personalized with the baby's name. Decorate the buffet table with the baby's name spelled with large wooden letters, and give the letters to the mom-to-be at the end of the party.

Favors

→ Give each guest a decorative rubber stamp that features the first letter of her last name. Wrap the stamp in cellophane and ribbon and attach a thank-you note.

→ Buy inexpensive trinkets whose names start with different letters. Wrap each trinket in cellophane and ribbon, and attach to each bundle a small tag card that features the first letter of the trinket's name.

→ Use fabric paint to stencil the first letters of guests' names on separate cloth napkins that have been folded into quarters. If you like, use the stenciled napkins as place cards.

Food

→ Alphabet soup fits this theme to the letter. Browse through cookbooks or surf the Internet to find a recipe that whets your appetite.

→ Cheese Spread Block

3 cups cooked chicken, diced
Two 8-ounce packages cream cheese, softened
2 cups Parmesan cheese, shredded
14-ounce can artichoke hearts, drained and diced
1 cup chopped pecans
1 tablespoon minced onion
1 tablespoon lemon juice
¼ teaspoon salt
¾ teaspoon seasoned pepper
8 green onion stems

Blend all the ingredients, except the green onion stems, together in a large bowl. Mold the mixture into a 9-by-5-inch loaf pan lined with plastic wrap. Cover the mixture with more plastic wrap and refrigerate overnight. Invert the pan onto a serving platter and remove the plastic wrap. To make a block shape, cut the loaf in half vertically. Place one half on top of the other. Use a knife to square the sides. Blanch the onion stems by dipping them into boiling water then quickly transferring them to ice water. Dry the stems between paper towels. Shape the stems into letters and attach them to the sides of the cheese spread block with toothpicks. Serve with crackers.

Napkin Alphabet Blocks

❧

Alphabet Soup

❧

Cheese Spread Block

→ Block Cake

Four 8-by-8-inch cakes, cooled (Prepare the cakes from packaged
mixes or double the recipe on page 115.)
Four 16-ounce cans white frosting (Use the
recipe on page 115 to make your own.)
Pastel candy-coated chocolate candies
Pastel-colored sugar sprinkles
Toy-shaped cookie cutter
8-by-8-inch cake board
6½-by-6½-inch cake board

Carefully remove the cakes from the pans. Wrap each
cake in plastic wrap and freeze them for 1 hour to make for easier cutting and fewer crumbs. Remove the plastic wrap, then
level the tops and sides of the cakes so they're the same size.
Place one cake on an 8-by-8-inch cake board and frost its top
with white frosting. Set another cake on top of the first and
frost its top. Set a 6½-by-6½-inch cake board on the cake stack.
(The cake board will give the cake stability.) Set the third cake
on top and frost its top. Top with the fourth cake. Frost the
entire cake to seal in crumbs. Divide the remaining frosting into
two portions. Tint one portion blue and the other pink. Frost
each side of the cake, alternating colors of frosting. Outline the
edges of the cake with the chocolate candies before the frosting
stiffens. Place the cookie cutter on top of the cake and pour
sugar sprinkles inside the shape. Remove the cookie cutter and
use a pastry bag (or see page 116 to make your own pastry bag)
to outline the shape with frosting. Decorate the sides of the
cake, if you like. This recipe makes 24 servings.

→ If you're short on time, bake and frost a plain sheet cake (or order
one from your local bakery). Top it with alphabet blocks that spell
the word *baby.* Or bake or buy a batch of cupcakes. Frost them
pink or blue, and top with sugar sprinkles and alphabet cereal.

Block Cake

Alphabet Sheet Cake

Pink or Blue, Hope Your Dreams Come True!

Today more and more couples learn the sex of their babies during pregnancy. But for those waiting until baby's birth, this shower theme is a perfect way to celebrate the mystery and keep everyone guessing.

Invitations

→ Write the following poem with pink and blue fine-tip markers on note cards:

> *Will it be pink or will it be blue?*
> *Just take your guess—choose one of these two.*
> *In pink or blue wrap your present tight.*
> *We will count them all to see who is right.*

Enclose lengths of narrow pink and blue ribbons, one of each per invitation. At the shower, tally the number of pink and blue ribbons to determine the sex of the baby.

Pink or Blue Ribbon Invitations

→ Make a button baby invitation by stitching a small two-hole pink button onto the front of a folded note card and stitching on a slightly larger two-hole blue button below the pink one. Use pink and blue thread, and position the pink button so the holes are horizontal and the blue button so the holes are vertical. Use a fine-tip marker to add facial features and body parts. Inside the note card write the following poem:

> *Whether it's pink or whether it's blue,*
> *I know that this is most certainly true:*
> *Cute as a button baby will be*
> *Just take a look at the family tree.*

Button Baby Invitations

→ Buy packets of flower seeds that feature the words *pink* or *blue* in their names. If the flower name includes the word *blue,* write party details on pink card stock, cut to fit onto the seed packets. If the flower name features *pink,* use blue card stock. Include a headline that reads, "Pink or Blue, Hope [mom-to-be's name]'s Dreams Come True!" Glue the cards in place. Mail the invitations in padded envelopes.

Decorations

→ In the invitations, ask guests to wear attire that's pink and/or blue. As revelers arrive, the party area will quickly be awash with the colors.

→ Lavishly decorate the party area in pink and blue. Display candles, balloons, and flowers in these hues. Blue iris, hyacinth, and agapanthus, as well as roses, lilies, and daisies, are all excellent choices for flowers. If you like, use four small clear bud vases for your table centerpiece. Stencil a letter on each vase with blue paint to spell the word *baby.* Fill the vases with pink flowers. (Or use pink paint and blue flowers.) Or fill a vase with pink and blue chocolate rosebuds (see page 75).

→ Cover the table with pink gingham fabric and use blue napkins. (Or use blue gingham fabric and pink napkins.) Use place mats that feature baby photos of the expectant parents. To make the place mats, photocopy the photos and glue those of the dad-to-be on blue card stock and those of the mom-to-be on pink card stock. Cover the place mats with clear contact paper.

Activities

→ Rally guests to take the Pink & Blue Challenge to see just how well they know the parents-to-be. Before the shower, ask the expectant couple the questions listed on page 131 (and other questions, if you like). Record their answers. At game time, divide the guests into pink and blue teams. Ask the pink team a question about the mom-to-be. If they answer it correctly, they earn a point and the chance to answer the next question. If they answer incorrectly, ask the blue team a question about the dad-to-be. When all the questions have been asked, award prizes to the team that's earned the most points.

→ Play Old Wives' Tales. See page 132 for a list of folktales that foretell the baby's sex. Photocopy the page as needed on pink or blue paper. Hand each player a page and pencil, and challenge them to guess the baby's sex for each folklore. Award a prize to the player who guesses correctly the most. If the mom-to-be is game, you might actually try a few of these "tests" on her just for fun.

→ Paint an equal number of clothespins pink and blue. Give one of each to every guest. Place a small clothesbasket on the other side of the room. After each guest has attempted to toss her clothespins in, count the number of both pink and blue clothespins that are in the basket. Majority wins in determining the sex of the baby.

→ This activity is another old wives' tale to learn the baby's sex, and it's carried out after the gift-opening. Tie together all the ribbons that wrapped the gifts. Tie a ring belonging to the mom-to-be to one end of the long ribbon, then wind the ribbon into a ball. Have the guests stand in a circle around the mom-to-be, give them the ribbon ball, and have them pass it around the circle and unwind it. Pay close attention to when the ring appears. If the guest presents the ring to the group in her right hand, then the mom-to-be can expect a girl. If she presents the ring in her left hand, expect a boy.

→ If the mom-to-be is willing to reveal or learn the baby's sex, stage an Ultrasound Screening for the last activity. Ask the mom-to-be to bring her latest ultrasound video or photo to the party, along with a medical professional's written conclusion of the baby's sex in an envelope. Show the ultrasound to the

Pink & Blue Challenge

❧

Old Wives' Tales

❧

*Pink & Blue
Clothespin Drop*

❧

Gift-Opening Forecast

❧

Ultrasound Screening

Baby Name Gifts

Secret Gift Pass

*Pink & Blue
Thank-You Notes*

*Pink & Blue
Signed Onesie*

guests and have them cast their votes for the baby's sex. Tally the votes, then open the envelope to reveal the results.

Gifts

→ Invite the guests to select gifts that correspond to their favorite boy's and girl's names. For example, the name *Jonah* might mean a toy whale, while *Crystal* might equal a pretty crystal frame. If you like, present the mom-to-be with a book of baby names.

→ For gift-opening fun, follow these instructions. Invite guests to wrap their gifts with pink or blue gift-wrap. Buy a small general gift (for example, a votive candle, bath beads, or a sachet) and gift-wrap it in pink or blue. At the gift opening, have the guests pass the small gift as the mom-to-be opens her presents. Each time she says thank you, it's time to pass the gift. Keep the activity a secret from the mom-to-be until she opens her last gift. Whoever is holding the passed gift at that time gets to take it home.

→ Upon arrival, give guests each a pink or blue crayon, a folded blank note card, and matching envelope. Ask the guests to draw a baby-related design on the front of their cards and self-address their envelopes. The mom-to-be will then have everything she needs to send thank-you notes.

→ Have guests sign their names on a white onesie with pink and blue fabric pens. Present the signed onesie to the mom-to-be with a promise to frame it for baby's nursery, if she likes.

Favors

→ Give guests pink- and blue-tinted bath crystals. Follow these instructions to make your own bath crystals:

Epsom salts
Red and blue food coloring
Essential oil in your favorite scent
Pint-size Mason jars with lids
Fabric squares in baby motif
Decorative ribbon

Pour the Epsom salts into two bowls. In one bowl, stir in drops of red food coloring until you get the desired pink shade. In the other bowl, stir in drops of blue food coloring. Stir a few drops of essential oil in both bowls. Pour the salts into the Mason jars, alternating layers of pink and blue salts. Before screwing on the lids, place a fabric square on top of each jar. Tie each lid with ribbon and attach a tag card that features these instructions: "Add ¼ cup of the mixture to a hot bath and enjoy!" If you like, fill some jars with pink bath salts and others with blue. Let guests choose their colored bath salts.

Pink & Blue
Bath Crystals

→ Offer guests pink and blue chocolate kiss rosebuds. Follow these instructions to make each rosebud:

2 chocolate kisses, wrapped
5-by-5-inch squares of pink and blue cellophane
18-inch length sturdy floral wire
Green floral tape
Silk rose leaves

Set the chocolate kisses on the cellophane square so their bottoms are touching. Gather up the corners of the cellophane and twist them together to secure. Use floral tape to attach the wrapped kisses to floral wire. Wrap the rest of the floral wire with floral tape, then use the tape to attach a silk rose leaf to the stem. Place the chocolate rosebuds in a vase with baby's breath, and the bouquet can double as a centerpiece.

Chocolate Kiss
Rosebuds

Food

→ In separate microwave-safe bowls, melt pink- and blue-tinted chocolate candies (available where cake-baking supplies are sold). Dip some pretzels in the pink melted chocolate and some pretzels in the blue. Transfer the pretzels to wax paper to cool. You can also drizzle the melted chocolate over popcorn and toss in some pink- and blue-coated chocolate candies for added color.

→ Have guests try these delicious cold soups.

Tickled Pink Strawberry Soup

*2 cups fresh strawberries, stemmed and sliced
1 cup orange juice
⅓ cup sour cream
⅓ cup honey*

Mix all the ingredients, except for ½ cup strawberry slices, in a blender. Refrigerate the mixture overnight to allow the flavors to blend. Pour the chilled soup into bowls just before serving and top each with strawberry slices. This recipe makes 4 servings.

Little Boy Blueberry Soup

*Two 12-ounce packages frozen blueberries, thawed
1 cup water
½ cup sugar
2 tablespoons lemon juice
Dash of ground cinnamon
Dash of ground cloves
⅔ cup plain yogurt
⅔ cup plus more sour cream
Oatmeal cookies (optional)*

Purée the blueberries with the water in a blender. Pour the mixture into a saucepan. Stir in the sugar, lemon juice, cinnamon, and cloves. Bring the mixture to boil. Cover the saucepan and simmer for 5 minutes on low heat. Pour the mixture into a bowl and refrigerate until chilled. Add the yogurt and ⅔ cup sour cream. Stir the soup and chill it again. To serve, ladle the soup into bowls. Use a pastry bag (see page 116 to make your own pastry bag) to top the soup with swirls of sour cream. If you like, top the soup with crumbled oatmeal cookies instead of sour cream. This recipe makes 6 servings.

→ Pink & Blue Bread Bites

15-ounce box quick bread mix
1 cup water
1 tablespoon vegetable oil
1 egg
4 ounces cream cheese, softened
2 tablespoons blueberry pie filling
2 tablespoons strawberry preserves
Red and blue food coloring
Fresh blueberries and sliced strawberries (optional)

Preheat your oven to 350°F. Coat a 15-by-10-by-1-inch jellyroll pan with nonstick spray. Line the pan with wax paper followed by more nonstick spray. Stir the bread mix with the water, oil, and egg until the mixture's moistened. Spread the batter evenly in the pan and bake for 12 minutes or until the bread springs back in the center when lightly touched. Cool the bread for 15 minutes before removing it from the pan. Remove the wax paper and cool the bread completely. Freeze the bread for 1 hour for easier cutting. Combine 2 ounces of cream cheese with the pie filling in one bowl, and combine the remaining cream cheese with the preserves in another bowl. To the first bowl add blue food coloring until you reach the desired blue shade. To the other bowl add red food coloring until you reach the desired pink shade. Remove the bread from the freezer. Cut shapes from it using baby-related cookie cutters (or cut out baby-related shapes from card stock, use them as templates, and cut around them with a sharp knife). Spread some shapes with the blue cream cheese mixture and some with the pink. If you like, garnish the shapes with fresh blueberries and strawberries. This recipe makes 18 servings.

Little Boy
Blueberry Soup

❧

Pink & Blue
Bread Bites

Pink & Blue Cake

→ Serve a Pink & Blue Cake. Prepare an 18-ounce package of white cake mix according to package instructions. Divide the batter equally into 2 bowls. Add a 3-ounce package of your favorite pink-colored gelatin to one bowl and a 3-ounce package of your favorite blue-colored gelatin to the other. Stir in red and blue food coloring to enhance the color, if you like. Pour each batter into a separate 9-inch pan. Bake the cakes according to package instructions, then let the cakes cool. Thaw a 12-ounce container of whipped topping. Spread the topping on top of one cake and set the second cake on top. Frost the entire cake with the remaining whipped topping. Refrigerate until serving. This recipe makes 12 servings.

SOMEBUNNY SPECIAL

Hop to it and plan a shower that's sure to please everybunny on your guest list.

Invitations

→ Write party details on tag cards and add a headline that reads, "Hop on over! We're celebrating the arrival of Somebunny Special!" Attach the cards to small toy bunnies and mail the invitations in small boxes.

→ Use the template on page 122 to cut bunny-shaped invitations from decorative paper. Write party details on the bunnies' backs. Tie decorative ribbon around each bunny's neck and glue a cotton ball tail in place. Mail the invitations in large envelopes.

→ Write party details on tag cards and tie the cards to carrots with raffia. Buy fake carrots from your local craft store or use real ones with stems. Hand-deliver the carrot invitations or mail them in padded envelopes.

Decorations

→ If weather permits, host the party in an outdoor garden. Or create a garden indoors by displaying garden rakes, trowels, watering cans, and as many plants and flowers as you have or your budget allows. Include some whimsical touches, like a sign that reads, "Mr. McGregor's Garden" and a scarecrow wearing Peter Rabbit's baby blue jacket and a pair of shoes. Add another sign that reads, "Bunnies Beware." Scatter plush and toy rabbits throughout the party area.

→ Welcome guests with a larger-than-life carrot. Buy a sapling (or invite the guests to contribute to the purchase) to commemorate baby's birth. From foam board, cut a carrot shape that's as tall as the sapling's trunk. Paint the carrot orange. When the paint has

Bunny-in-a-Box Invitations

❦

Bunny Invitations

❦

Carrot Invitations

❦

Garden Setting

❦

Carrot Tree

dried, prop the carrot against the tree trunk. To secure, wrap clear fishing line around the carrot and tie in back. The foliage will become the carrot's stem. Following the party, volunteer to plant the tree in the mom-to-be's yard.

→ Adorn tables with bunny pot centerpieces. For each centerpiece, paint a clay pot pink or blue. When the paint has dried, glue two googly eyes onto the pot and glue on a white pom pom for the bunny's nose. Use a marker to draw on a mouth and whiskers. Cut bunny ears from coordinating colors of craft foam. Fill the pot with candy or flowers, and glue the ears in place.

Activities

→ Play Somebunny Famous. Photocopy the list of scrambled names of famous bunnies on page 133. Give the list and a pencil to each player and have the players race to unscramble the names. Award a book about one of these celebrated carrot-crunchers to the first guest to correctly unscramble the names.

→ Play Hopping Down the Bunny Trail, an exciting game that's somewhere between charades and Name That Tune. Write the titles of beloved children's songs, like "Here Comes Peter Cotton Tail," on separate slips of paper. (See page 134 for more inspiration.) Ask players to take turns acting out song titles for the group. Award a baby carrot to the first player who correctly identifies each song title. The player with the most carrots wins a prize.

→ Divide the guests into equal teams for a game of Bunny Tail Transfer. Give each team a blindfold, a spoon, an empty bowl, and a bowl filled with bunny tails (cotton balls). Have the first player from each team put on the blindfold. Set the timer for one minute and have the first players transfer as many bunny tails as possible from one bowl to the other using only their spoons. When time is up, record how many bunny tails each player successfully transferred. Play continues until every team member has had a turn. The team that collectively transfers the most bunny tails wins prizes.

Gifts

→ Invite guests each to bring a copy of a favorite bunny tale for baby's library. Suggest they also choose gifts that correspond to the books.

→ Using manicure scissors, cut beautiful watercolor illustrations from an old copy of Beatrix Potter's *The Tale of Peter Rabbit.* Decoupage the cutouts onto a photo frame, lampshade, chair, or other item for baby's nursery.

→ Boo-boo bunnies are magical creatures known to make boo-boos disappear. The mom-to-be is sure to find them helpful when her future toddler gets a boo-boo. Follow these instructions to make each bunny:

Scissors
Lightweight washcloth
Sturdy rubber band
Glue
Two 10-millimeter googly eyes
Two ½-inch white pom poms
Embroidery floss
Decorative ribbon
Plastic ice cube (optional)

Cut any tags off the washcloth. Lay the washcloth flat with one corner pointing toward you. Roll that corner tightly to the center. Tightly roll the opposite corner to the center. Fold the washcloth in half so the unrolled corners meet and the rolled corners are on the inside. Hold the washcloth at the middle with one hand and use the other hand to pull down each free end until it meets the fold. Wrap a rubber band around the entire washcloth

Bunny Tail Transfer

❦

Bunny Tales

❦

Bunny Decoupage

❦

Boo-Boo Bunnies

about 1 inch from the top of the end opposite the fold. Turn the washcloth so the part above the rubber band faces you. This will be the bunny's face. Glue on googly eyes, a pom pom nose, and embroidery floss whiskers. Glue a pom pom tail in place on the fold. Cover the rubber band with decorative ribbon. If you like, insert a plastic ice cube in the center of the bunny.

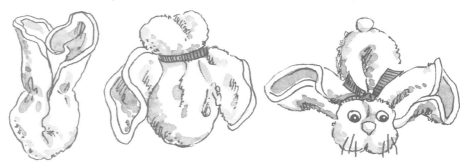

Attach to the bunny a tag card that features the following poem:

My name is Boo-Boo Bunny.
Put ice inside my tummy.
Place me on your boo-boo tight—
Everything will be all right!

(Please note that boo-boo bunnies should be used only with adult supervision as they contain small parts that can pose a choking hazard to small children.)

Favors

→ Make bunny sachets for the guests. For each sachet, follow these instructions:
Two 6-by-7-inch felt pieces
Scissors
Matching thread
Needle or sewing machine
Fiberfill

Boo-Boo Bunnies

Bunny Sachets

Potpourri
1-inch white pom pom
Decorative ribbon

Stack the felt pieces and use the template on page 122 to cut bunny shapes from both. Stitch the two shapes together, leaving about a 3-inch opening at the bottom. Stuff the bunny with fiberfill and potpourri, then stitch the opening closed. Stitch a pom pom tail in place. Tie a ribbon around the bunny's neck along with a thank-you note.

→ Give guests bunny pot favors. See page 80 to make the bunny pots, but use small pots that can double as place cards. Fill the pots with jellybeans.

Food

→ Scatter small baskets of baby carrots around the party area for guests to nibble on. Carve out the center of a cabbage and fill it with vegetable dip. Set the cabbage in the center of a vegetable tray.

→ Bunny Bread Dip Bowl
Large round bread loaf
4-inch bun
Two 2-inch dinner rolls
Toothpicks
3 raisins
Six 4-inch pieces of chive
Large baguette
Cauliflower floret

Carve out the center of the round bread loaf to make a bowl, leaving at least 1 inch of bread on the sides and bottom. This will be the bunny's body. Attach the bun to the body with toothpicks to form the head. Slit to insert raisin eyes and nose. Use a toothpick to poke holes to insert chive whiskers. Cut the baguette in half to form the bunny's ears. Attach the ears to the head with toothpicks. Attach the dinner rolls in place with toothpicks to make the bunny's feet. Attach the cauliflower tail in place with toothpicks, and fill the bunny bread bowl with your favorite vegetable dip.

→ Cheesy Bunny Appetizers

Two 8-ounce packages cream cheese, softened
Packet of ranch dip mix
Large cucumber, sliced
20 raisins, cut in half
Large red pepper, cut into 20 tiny triangles
Eighty ½-inch pieces of chive
5 baby carrots, quartered lengthwise

Blend the cream cheese with the dip mix in a small bowl and refrigerate for 3 hours or until firm. Roll the mixture into 20 equal-size balls. Decorate each ball with 2 raisin eyes, a red pepper triangle nose, 4 chive whiskers, and 2 carrot ears. Return the bunnies to the refrigerator. Cut the cucumber into 20 equal slices. Place each bunny on a cucumber slice to serve. This recipe makes 20 servings.

→ Bunny Cake

Two 9-inch round cakes, cooled (Prepare the
*   cakes from a packaged mix or use the*
*   recipe on page 115.)*
Two 16-ounce cans white frosting
*   (Use the recipe on page 115*
*   to make your own.)*
2¼ cups coconut
Red food coloring
3 large gumdrops, 2 blue M&M's, red
*   string licorice, and pink and blue jellybeans*

Carefully remove the cakes from the pans. Wrap each cake in plastic wrap and freeze them for 1 hour to make for easier cutting and fewer crumbs. Remove the plastic wrap, then level the tops of the cakes with a knife. Set one cake on the center of a cake board. This will be the bunny's head. Cut bunny ears from the other cake. The remaining cake will be the bunny's bow tie. Position the ears and bow tie around the bunny's head. Frost the bunny cake entirely with white frosting. Use red food coloring to tint ¼ cup of coconut pastel pink (see page 45 for instructions). Sprinkle everything but the bow tie with the remaining white coconut. Sprinkle the pink-tinted coconut on the insides of the bunny's ears. Add a gumdrop nose and eyes. Top each eye with a blue M&M and use string licorice to make a mouth and whiskers. Scatter jellybean polka dots on the bow tie. This recipe makes 12 servings.

→ If you're short on time, a carrot cake purchased from your local bakery will fit the bill.

Bunny Cake

Carrot Cake

SHAKE, RATTLE, & ROLL

Shake it up, baby, and let the good times roll with this great theme!

Invitations

→ Write party details on tag cards and attach the cards to inexpensive baby rattles. Mail the invitations in small boxes.

→ Make paper rattle invitations. For each invitation, cut two circles, each 4 inches in diameter, from decorative card stock. Cut a rattle-handle shape from the card stock. Write party details on one of the circles. Pour a small amount of rice on the center of the other circle, and squeeze glue around its circumference. Set the rattle handle in the glue at the bottom of the circle, and press the other circle on top of the first. Add a small decorative bow to the top of the rattle's handle. Mail the invitations in large envelopes.

→ Decorate the front of folded plain card stock invitations with an embroidered rattle. Lightly pencil a rattle shape on the card front and use a thumbtack to punch holes along the design at approximately ⅛-inch intervals. Backstitch with embroidery floss through the holes (see page 54 for instructions).

Decorations

→ Display a rattle tree centerpiece. Find a sturdy, 18- to 24-inch tree branch that has many smaller branches. Remove any leaves or debris and paint the entire branch a pastel color. When the paint has dried, anchor the branch in a large flower pot filled with rocks. Hide the pot with a baby blanket. Hang small rattles and baby toys from the branches with string. Or if you like, invite guests to bring such items to the shower and display them on the tree.

→ Grow a crop of rattles in a decorative basket. Don't let the idea intimidate you. The rattles are easy to "sow," but it will take a little planning. About three weeks before the party, line the bottom of your basket with plastic. Fill the basket with potting soil and generously plant grass seed. Then a little sunshine and water are all you need. Mist the soil with water frequently to avoid drowning the seeds, and your basket should be full of grass by party time. Wire rattles to wooden picks and stick them in the grass to look like flowers. Tie a decorative bow on the basket's handle. If necessary, you may substitute real grass with a silk variety from the floral department of your local craft store.

→ On your buffet table, display anything round or on wheels, including balls, pull toys, and baby carriages. Display a collection of baby carriages made from ordinary baskets. They're perfect for housing everything from napkins to muffins. Follow these instructions to make each carriage basket:

Scissors
Card stock
Rectangular basket with handle
Glue gun
Fabric in a baby motif
Lace (optional)
Felt scraps

Rattle Tree Centerpiece

❦

Rattle Garden

❦

Baby Carriage Baskets

Cut the card stock to form an archway over one half of the basket. Glue one edge of the card stock onto the basket handle. Cover the card stock with fabric to form a carriage hood, gluing the fabric to the basket edges and handle. If you like, glue lace around the edge of the carriage hood and basket edges. To finish, glue on four wheels cut from felt.

Activities

→ Challenge guests to a game of What's in Baby's Bag? Place a combination of common and hard-to-identify baby items (like a cotton swab or a medicine dropper) in separate paper bags. Close the bags and number them. Give the players paper and pencils. Circulate the bags around the room and instruct players that they may shake, rattle, or roll the bags to help them guess the contents—but no peeking! Have the players record their answers. Award the player who correctly identifies the most items with a gift certificate for a milkshake.

→ Play Double Dice Roll. Buy a variety of inexpensive gifts, like votive candles or bath beads, and include a few gag gifts. Wrap all the gifts. At game time, have the guests sit in a circle. Set the gifts in the center of the circle. Drop a pair of dice into each of two empty baby wipe containers, and give the containers to two guests sitting on opposite sides of the circle. Ask these guests to shake the containers and roll out the dice. If a guest doesn't roll doubles, she must pass the dice to the guest on her right. If she does roll doubles, she gets to pick a gift from the pile before passing the dice on. The fun begins when all the prizes are claimed and guests get to steal from one another upon rolling doubles. When the game is called, each guest gets to open and keep the gifts in her possession.

→ Play Shake That Tune. Gather a variety of children's toy instruments and rattles. Write the list of children's song titles on page 134 (and other titles, if you like) on separate slips of paper. Divide the guests into pairs and have each pair draw a paper slip. Let the pairs take turns performing their selections in front of the group, using the provided instruments. At least one guest in the pair must play an instrument, and the other may simultaneously pantomime the song. Pairs earn a point if someone correctly identifies their song titles within an allotted amount of time. The guest who correctly guesses the song title earns two points for her team. When all the pairs have performed their selections, the pair with the most points wins prizes.

Gifts

→ Invite guests to bring gifts for baby that shake, rattle, or roll. Obvious gifts include rattles and balls, but other appropriate gifts could include CDs of lively children's tunes that the future toddler can shake and dance to.

→ Save scraps of gift-wrap from the shower and decoupage them onto a wooden frame. Glue on a rattle or two. Present the treasured keepsake to the guest of honor along with a favorite photo from the festivities.

Favors

→ Give guests small items from a dollar store that you can shake, rattle, or roll. Try salt- and peppershakers or back massagers. Wrap the items in cellophane and ribbon.

→ Give guests chocolate-covered Oreo rattles. To make the rattles, stick the ends of Popsicle sticks into the fillings of separate Double Stuf Oreos. Melt semisweet chocolate chips over low heat or in a microwave. Add small amounts of vegetable oil to the melted chocolate until it's the consistency of pancake syrup. Spoon the chocolate over the cookies, making sure to cover the

Shake That Tune

*Gifts That Shake,
Rattle, or Roll*

Rattle Frame

*Favors to Shake,
Rattle, or Roll*

❧

Oreo Rattles

tops of the sticks as well. (A 12-ounce package of chocolate chips will cover about 20 Double Stuf Oreos.) Place the cookies on a wax-paper-covered baking sheet and refrigerate them to set the chocolate. Once the chocolate has hardened, decorate the cookies to look like rattles by piping a contrasting color of chocolate from a pastry bag (see page 116 to make your own pastry bag). Chocolate wafers in a variety of colors are sold along with baking supplies.

→ Try the following recipe to make guests Popcorn Ball Rattles:

6 packages microwave popcorn, popped (hulls removed)
2 sticks butter
Two 16-ounce packages marshmallows
Red or blue food coloring (optional)
22 candy sticks (Pink- or blue-striped sticks would be darling.)

Pour the popcorn into a large bowl. Microwave the butter with the marshmallows until melted. If desired, use the food coloring to tint the mixture pink or blue. Drizzle the mixture over the popcorn. Mold the popcorn into balls, and insert a candy stick into the center of each ball to form the rattle's handle. Lay the popcorn balls on wax paper to set. Cover the popcorn balls in pink or blue cellophane and tie with ribbon. This recipe makes 22 Popcorn Ball Rattles.

Food

→ Cheesy Rattle

Four 8-ounce packages cream cheese, softened
Two 8-ounce cans crushed pineapple, drained
½ cup chopped green pepper
4 tablespoons chopped green onion
4 teaspoons seasoned salt
Red or blue food coloring (optional)
Dowel rod
Decorative ribbon

Blend together the cream cheese, pineapple, green pepper, onion, and salt. If you like, use food coloring to tint the mixture pink or blue. Form the mixture into 2 balls. Wrap each ball in plastic wrap and refrigerate them overnight. To serve, remove the plastic wrap, place the cheese balls on a tray, and set a dowel rod wrapped in ribbon between them horizontally. Cover the tray with crackers.

→ Watermelon Baby Carriage

Large watermelon
Toothpicks
Large grapefruit

Set the watermelon on a dampened dishtowel. Beginning at the middle of one end, cut through the watermelon horizontally roughly two-thirds the way to the other end. Beginning at the top of the watermelon directly above where you ended the first cut, cut down through the fruit until you reach the first cut. Remove the cut portion, scrape off the fruit, and carve a curved handlebar from the rind. Use a melon baller to scoop out the fruit from the watermelon. Attach the carriage handle in place with toothpicks. Slice the grapefruit into 4 slices to make carriage wheels and attach the wheels in place with toothpicks. Fill the watermelon with fruit salad (see the following recipe) and serve.

→ Fruit Salad

2 cantaloupes
2 honeydews
Watermelon balls from carved melon (See previous recipe.)
4 cups strawberries, sliced
2 cups seedless grapes, halved
½ cup sugar
½ cup lime juice
¼ cup lemon juice
Orange, 2 sliced grapes, cloves, and pacifier (optional)

Cheesy Rattle

Watermelon Baby Carriage

Fruit Salad

Use a melon baller to remove the fruit from the cantaloupes and honeydews, and place the fruit in a large bowl. Add the watermelon balls, strawberries, and grapes. Stir in the sugar and lime and lemon juices. Cover the salad and refrigerate. To serve, pour the fruit salad into a watermelon carriage (see the previous recipe). To finish, use toothpicks to stick 2 sliced grapes into an orange to make eyes in a baby's head. Use toothpicks to stick cloves on the eyes for pupils. Carve a mouth in the baby's face and stick in a pacifier. Place the baby's head in the finished fruit carriage.

→ Rattle Cake

Four 9-inch round cakes, cooled (Prepare the cakes from packaged mixes or double the recipe on page 115.)
Four 16-ounce cans white frosting (Use the recipe on page 115 to make your own.)
Tube from paper towel roll
Food coloring
Decorative ribbon bow

Frost the tops of 2 cakes. Stack a cake on each frosted cake. Place the 2 stacked cakes side by side on a cake board, leaving enough space to lay the tube between them horizontally. Frost both cakes and the tube completely. Use food coloring to tint the remaining frosting. Place the tinted frosting in a pastry bag (or see page 116 to make your own pastry bag), and decorate the cakes to look like a rattle. Set a decorative ribbon bow on the handle. This recipe makes 24 servings.

A Star Is Born

This starry celebration is sure to be heavenly for all who attend.

Invitations

→ Pour glitter or shiny confetti on small cellophane squares. Tie the bundles tightly with decorative ribbon. Attach to each bundle a card stock star cutout that reads, "Please sprinkle this stardust and make a wish for Baby [baby's last name)]!" Write party details on the other side of the cutout.

→ Paint small wood stars (available at your local craft store) a solid light color. From card stock cut diapers that can be folded around the stars and fastened in front with a diaper pin. Write party details on the diapers. Use a fine-tip marker to draw facial features on the star's top point and mail the invitations in padded envelopes with star-shaped confetti enclosed.

→ Write party details on the inside of folded midnight blue card stock invitations. Use a glow-in-the-dark pen to draw a star on the front of the card or decorate the front with metallic stickers and glitter puffy paint.

Decorations

→ If the mom-to-be agrees, hold the shower in the evening and let twinkle lights strung from the ceiling bathe your party in starlight. Swag the strings of lights with tulle fabric to look like clouds. Also hang from the ceiling cardboard star cutouts, each covered with aluminum foil or decorated with silver paint and glitter.

→ Line the sidewalk or decorate your party area with these easy-to-make tin can luminaries:

Stardust Invitations

❦

Baby Star Invitations

❦

Night Sky Invitations

❦

Starlight Décor

❦

Tin Can Luminaries

Permanent marker
Large empty tin cans (labels removed)
Towel
Hammer
Nail
Votive candles

Tin Can Luminaries

Use a marker to outline celestial shapes in dots all around the cans. Fill the cans with water and freeze them overnight. Working with one can at a time, remove it from the freezer and lay it on its side on the towel. Place the nail on each dot of the design and hammer it through until it hits the ice. (The ice will keep the can from collapsing.) Once the entire pattern is complete, allow the ice to melt and pour out the water. Dry the insides of luminaries before inserting the candles. Remember to never leave burning candles unattended.

Heavenly Buffet Table

→ Replicate the heavens on your buffet table. Cover the table with a solid white tablecloth. Sprinkle star-shaped confetti or celestial shapes cut from card stock all across the tabletop. Cover the table again with sheer white fabric. Cover large sturdy boxes with white batting and set them on the table. Set food platters on the boxes and scatter fiberfill clouds between the boxes. Hang moon and star card stock cutouts from the ceiling above the table. If hosting the party in the evening, place a small table lamp (minus the lampshade) beneath the table to set the table aglow.

Plush Animal Angels

→ Assemble a choir of plush animal angels. To make angel wings, pinch together the long sides of small iridescent cellophane rectangles to make bow tie shapes. Wrap thread around the pinched areas to secure the shapes. Attach the cellophane wings to plush animals with a stitch of thread. The wings can easily be removed with a scissors' snip.

Activities

→ Divide guests into teams to take the Celestial Challenge. Write each team's list (see page 134) on separate slips of paper. Give at least one slip of paper to each teammate. One player from the first team has 30 seconds to try and get her teammates to guess the word on her slip—without saying the assigned word in any form. If the team correctly identifies her word in time, it earns a point. If not, the other team may make a guess, and if correct it earns two points. Alternate play between the teams until all of the slips have been used. Award small packages of Starburst candies to the team with the most points.

→ Stage your own version of Star Search in which teams write new lyrics to lullabies. Divide the guests into teams. Provide each team a tape or CD player and a recording of an instrumental lullaby. The objective is for teams to write original lyrics to their assigned songs. When finished, have each team perform its song for the mom-to-be. Award prizes for the funniest lyrics, the best performance, and so on.

→ Play a star-studded version of the Name Game. Set a timer and have players race to write down celestial titles under these categories: songs, books, films, and TV shows (for example, "Moondance," *The Sun Also Rises, A Star Is Born,* and *Star Search).* Award a prize to the player who comes up with the most titles.

Gifts

→ Invite guests to contribute funds to register a star in baby's name. You can reach the International Star Registry by calling 800-282-3333 or by visiting their web site at www.starregistry.com. The company will send a beautiful parchment certificate that features the star's name and its telescopic coordinates. Attach a tag card to the certificate that reads, "Baby, you're a star!"

Celestial Challenge

❧

Lullaby Star Search

❧

Star Name Game

❧

Star Registry

→ In the invitations, assign each guest to bring a celestial gift in one of these categories: moon, sun, stars, clouds, and Milky Way. For more inspiration, see the items listed in Celestial Challenge on page 134.

→ Help the baby wish upon a star. Use a fabric pen to decorate a crib sheet with celestial shapes. Ask guests to each add a sweet dreams message before leaving the shower.

Favors

→ Give guests Twinkle, Twinkle, Little Star votive candleholders. To make each candleholder, use midnight blue acrylic paint to cover a small terra cotta pot. When the paint is dry, use a gold paint pen to decorate the pot with stars and to add the phrase "Twinkle, Twinkle, Little Star" around its rim. Drop in a scented votive candle and wrap the pot in cellophane and ribbon. Attach a tag card that features the classic nursery rhyme and a note of thanks.

→ Give guests a taste of heaven. Place wrapped Starburst candies and bite-size Milky Way candy bars into pyramid favor boxes (see page 120 to make the boxes). Use a fine-tip marker to decorate the boxes with stars.

Food

→ Use a star-shaped cookie cutter to cut stars from a variety of cheeses. Serve the cheesy star slices with crackers.

→ Offer a Starry Fruit Platter. Set a bowl of fruit dip (see the following recipe) on the center of a large platter. Remove the rind and seeds from watermelon slices and cut the fruit into triangles. Stack the watermelon triangles around the bowl of fruit dip so they point out to create a star shape. Place other cut fruit on the platter.

→ Fruit Dip

8-ounce can crushed pineapple
3-ounce package instant coconut cream pudding mix
¾ cup milk
½ cup sour cream
1 teaspoon poppy seeds

Mix all the ingredients in a blender for 1 minute. Refrigerate the fruit dip for several hours to allow the flavors to blend. This recipe makes 2 cups of fruit dip.

→ Prepare sugar cookie dough (use the recipe on page 117 to make you own). Use a star-shaped cookie cutter to cut the dough into stars. Bake the cookies according to the recipe's instructions, then let the cookies cool. Dip one half of each cookie into melted chocolate. Or cover the cookies with pastel frosting and top them with shiny sugar sprinkles. If you like, leave the cookies unfrosted and serve them with fruit dip (see the previous recipe).

→ Man in the Moon Cake

13-by-9-inch cake, cooled (Prepare the cake from a packaged mix
or use the recipe on page 115.)
Two 16-ounce cans white frosting (Use the recipe on page 115
to make your own.)
18-ounce package refrigerated sugar cookie dough (Use the recipe
on page 117 to make your own.)
Yellow, red, and blue food coloring
Tube of brown decorating frosting

Carefully remove the cake from the pan. Wrap the cake in plastic wrap and freeze it for 1 hour to make for easier cutting and fewer crumbs. Remove the plastic wrap, then cut the cake lengthwise into a crescent moon shape. Place the cutout on a cake board. Roll the cookie dough on a floured surface. Use a star-shaped cookie cutter to cut stars from the dough and place the shapes on a lightly greased baking sheet. Bake the cookies

Fruit Dip

❧

Sugar Cookie Stars

❧

Man in the Moon Cake

according to the recipe's instructions. Cool the cookies on wire racks. Use ½ cup of frosting from one can to frost a nightcap on the crescent moon. Tint the rest of the frosting in that can light yellow and use it to frost the rest of the moon. Tint the other can of frosting either pink or blue (or a combination of the two) and use it to decorate the star cookies and add stripes to the moon's nightcap. Add a closed eye, nose, and mouth to the moon cake with brown decorating frosting. Surround the cake with star cookies and pipe a string of brown frosting *Z*s on the cake board near the moon's mouth. This recipe makes 18 servings.

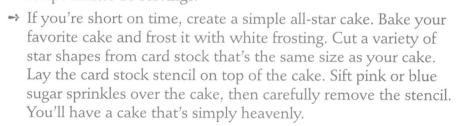

→ If you're short on time, create a simple all-star cake. Bake your favorite cake and frost it with white frosting. Cut a variety of star shapes from card stock that's the same size as your cake. Lay the card stock stencil on top of the cake. Sift pink or blue sugar sprinkles over the cake, then carefully remove the stencil. You'll have a cake that's simply heavenly.

→ Make your favorite dessert recipe and adorn the treats with chocolate garnishes in moon or star shapes (see page 117 for instructions). For fun, place a star-shaped sticker on the bottom of one of the dessert plates. Award a door prize to the guest who spots the star on her plate.

Man in the Moon Cake

❦

All-Star Cake

❦

Chocolate Star Garnishes

ONCE UPON A TIME...

This party is sure to have guests celebrating happily ever after.

Invitations

→ Send storybook invitations. Buy inexpensive copies of classic fairy tales. Write party details on decorative bookplates and stick a bookplate on the inside cover of each book. Mail the books in padded envelopes.

→ Cut shield shapes from gray card stock. Decorate one side of the shields with markers, paint, or glued-on fabric scraps. Write the party details on the other side.

→ Send bookmark invitations. Cut long rectangles from card stock and punch a hole near a short edge of each one. On one side of each rectangle, write the following poem:

> Please bring a small book
> In lieu of a card.
> It need not cost much,
> Soft cover or hard.

On the other side write the party details. Decorate the bookmarks with markers or paint pens. Thread a ribbon tassel through each hole.

Decorations

→ Welcome guests with a large paper banner that reads, "Once upon a Time..." Lay a length of inexpensive red fabric from the door to the party area. (Be careful it's not a slipping hazard.) Decorate a high-back chair to make a throne for the mom-to-be. Truly make her queen for the day by having her wear an inexpensive tiara.

Storybook Invitations

❦

Shield Invitations

❦

Bookmark Invitations

❦

Royal Décor

→ For a centerpiece, cut a tri-fold castle façade from a display board. Paint it to look as though it's made of stone. At the top, attach a card stock banner flag that reads, "Once upon a Time…" Set a collection of classic fairy tale books between a pair of baby-motif bookends. Present the collection to the mom-to-be following the shower.

→ Transform your party area into the setting of the classic fairy tale *Hansel and Gretel.* Line the walkway or the party area with giant lollipops. To make each lollipop, paint a dowel rod a bright color and top it with a Styrofoam disc wrapped in colorful cellophane. Top your table with a brightly colored tablecloth, and gather the cloth's edges around each table leg with colorful curling ribbon and bunches of lollipops. For a centerpiece, make an edible gingerbread house from a kit or construct one from cardboard and puffy paint. Bake gingerbread men cookies and decorate them with pink and blue frosting diapers. Prop the cookies on either side of the house. Glue green gumdrops all over Styrofoam cones to make trees. Use candy bracelets or Saf-T-Pops suckers as napkin rings and hang pink and blue candy canes from the punch bowl.

→ For an appropriate ambience for your storybook shower, host the celebration at your local library. Invite guests to come dressed as favorite storybook characters.

Activities

→ Play Little Red Riding Hood's Basket. Write the list of fairy tales on page 135 on separate slips of paper. Place the paper slips in a small basket. Gather a collection of props that correspond with the fairy tales on the slips, and put the props in another basket. At game time, divide the guests into two teams. Have a member from one team draw a slip and silently act out the fairy tale for her teammates, using the props from the basket. If her team correctly identifies the tale within one minute, it earns one point. If not, the other team may make a guess, and if correct it earns two points. Alternate play between the two teams until all the fairy tales have been acted out. The team with the most points wins prizes.

→ Make a fairy godmothers necklace. Give each guest two decorative beads. Knot the end of a length of thin decorative cord. Seat the guests in a circle and have them take turns stringing one of their beads onto the cord with a wish for the mom-to-be. Then go around the circle again and have them add their second beads with a wish for baby. Tie the ends of the cord together to make a necklace. Suggest that mom-to-be keep the necklace nearby during labor and delivery so her fairy godmothers' wishes come true.

→ Challenge guests to a game of Famous Story Lines. Photocopy the list on page 136 and distribute the copies with pencils to the players. At your mark, have the players race to write down the tales from which the famous lines have been pulled. The player to first accomplish this task wins a gift certificate to a local bookstore or a copy of one of the tales.

Gifts

→ Invite guests to each bring a copy of a favorite childhood book to build baby's library. Or if you like, invite guests to contribute funds to purchase a bookcase that matches the nursery décor.

→ Make a set of bookends from a pair of plush animals. Cut a hole in the back seam of each animal and remove some stuffing. Insert a few marbles to add weight. Stitch the seam closed. To prevent the bookend from slipping, paint the animal's bottom with puffy paint.

→ Invite special faraway friends or relatives to create a timeless gift for baby by recording themselves reading a classic childhood story.

Fairy Godmothers Necklace

❦

Famous Story Lines

❦

Stock Baby's Library

❦

Plush Animal Bookends

❦

Record a Story

Autographed Storybook

Handmade Bookmarks

Bookstore Gift Certificates

Fairy Tale Favors

Fairy Tale Buffet

Hansel and Gretel's Peppermint Parfait Pie

→ Look for children's author appearances at local bookstores and schools. A personalized edition of any book for baby is a keepsake. Or have each guest sign a hardcover edition of a book of classic fairy tales to make a personalized shower memento.

Favors

→ Give handmade bookmarks (see Bookmark Invitations on page 99) to thank guests for helping you mark baby's birth.

→ Present guests gift certificates in small amounts to a local bookstore. Roll the certificates and tie each with ribbon to look like a scroll.

→ Give guests favors that correspond with fairy tales. For example, Jack's magic beans could be jellybeans wrapped in cellophane and tied with ribbon. Or packets of pea seeds could represent the Princess and the Pea. Attach a note of thanks to each favor.

Food

→ Prepare a fairy tale buffet. At the beginning of the buffet table, set a sign that reads, "Once upon a Time There Was a Delicious Storybook Buffet." Set a sign that reads, "The End" at the other end of the buffet table. In between the signs, serve items that correspond to classic storybooks, like bean salad as a tribute to Jack and the Beanstalk, an apple side dish to salute Snow White, or barbequed pork in honor of the Three Little Pigs. See pages 25–26 to find recipes appropriate to celebrate the Princess and the Pea. End your feast with one of the following sweet treats.

→ Hansel and Gretel's Peppermint Parfait Pie

1 ounce unsweetened chocolate
1 teaspoon clear vanilla extract
14-ounce can sweetened condensed milk
9-inch graham cracker piecrust
8-ounce package cream cheese, softened
2 teaspoons peppermint extract

Red or blue food coloring
8-ounce container frozen whipped topping, thawed
Peppermint candies

Melt the chocolate with the vanilla and ½ cup of condensed milk in a small saucepan over low heat. Spread the mixture onto the bottom of the piecrust. In a bowl, beat the cream cheese until it's fluffy. Blend in the remaining condensed milk, peppermint extract, and enough red or blue food coloring to reach the desired shade. Fold in the cream cheese mixture with the whipped topping, and spoon the filling into the piecrust. Chill the pie overnight. Garnish it with peppermint candies. This recipe makes 8 servings.

→ Castle Cake

Two 9-by-5-inch cakes, cooled (Prepare the cakes from a packaged
*   mix or use the recipe on page 115.)*
4 ounces white chocolate
2 sugar ice cream cones
Pink or blue sugar sprinkles
Red or blue food coloring
Two 16-ounce cans white frosting (Use the recipe on page 115
*   to make your own.)*
22 small gumdrops
10 large gumdrops
Fruit snack rolls
Blue-tinted coconut (See page 45 for instructions.)
3-inch pretzel sticks

Carefully remove the cakes from the pans. Wrap each cake in plastic wrap, and freeze them for 1 hour to make for easier cutting and fewer crumbs. To make the castle spires, melt the white chocolate and use a spatula to thoroughly coat both ice cream cones with the melted chocolate. Sprinkle colored sugar on the cones. Set the cones pointed ends up on wax paper. Refrigerate the cones to set the chocolate. Remove the plastic

Castle Cake

wrap from the cakes, and level them with a knife. Place one cake on the center of a cake board. Cut the other cake in half vertically and stand one half on each side of the whole cake. Attach the cake pieces with toothpicks and a dab of frosting. Use the food coloring to tint the frosting a desired shade of pink or blue. Frost the entire castle cake. Top each vertical cake piece with an ice cream cone spire. Surround each spire with 10 small gumdrops and top each with the remaining small gumdrops. Write best wishes for baby on small banner flags cut from construction paper, and glue the flags onto toothpicks. Insert the toothpick banners into the gumdrops on top of the spires. Use large gumdrops to form battlements along the top of the castle's main section. Carve window and door shapes from fruit snack rolls and press them in place on the front of the castle. Surround the castle with blue-tinted coconut "water" and add a drawbridge made from pretzel sticks set side by side. This recipe makes 16 servings.

More Fun Shower Ideas

In this section you'll find great ideas for throwing a party that's tailored for special circumstances. Get the dad-to-be involved by throwing a Couples' Shower with hilarious coed activities. Host a Sip 'n' See and let the family debut their new arrival to well-wishers. Send a shower by mail to an expectant friend who lives in the next town or the next country. Throw a casual, scaled-down Sprinkle for a mom-to-be who's had a full-scale shower or two. Make an expectant big brother or sister feel special by staging a Sibling Celebration. You can incorporate any of these ideas into any of the shower themes in this book to make your celebration extraordinary.

Couples' Shower

The mom-to-be isn't the only one responsible for baby's arrival. The dad-to-be has his fair share of responsibility, too. So throw a celebration that honors both parents-to-be. You can adapt any shower theme in this book for a coed guest list. Another idea is to base your celebration on a favorite hobby of the parents-to-be, like camping, golfing, or traveling.

Since the guest list may be large, consider scaling back on the decorations, favors, and menu if you're working with a tight budget. Invite couples, but not exclusively. Single friends are welcome, and if you invite enough of them, they can pair up for some activities. The following are shower activities that are sure to be a hit (not to mention a hoot) with women *and* men.

Coed Activities

Bobbing for Pacifiers

→ Play Bobbing for Pacifiers. This activity could prove refreshing at a summertime barbecue baby shower. Fill a large washtub with water, pour in plenty of pacifiers, and let the players bob for pacifiers. As an inexpensive alternative, use nipples from baby bottles instead of pacifiers.

Shooting Poops

→ Make the mom- and dad-to-be team captains in this unique free throw competition. Divide the guests equally into two teams. Set two diaper pails a designated distance from a free-throw line. Give each team five diapers that have been stained with mustard or melted chocolate. Instruct the team members to take turns shooting all the balled-up diapers into the team's diaper pail. The team that collectively gets the most "poops" in its pail wins prizes.

Pregnant Papas

→ Here's a game for men who've wondered what it feels like to be pregnant. At game time, each player will run through an obstacle course of tasks that many expectant moms in their third trimesters find challenging, such as tying their shoes, picking up pennies from the floor, and reclining then getting up from a bed or sofa. Place a bowling ball or about 20 pounds of melons in a backpack and have the first player put it on so the weight rests on his belly. (If necessary, stabilize the backpack by tying a long scarf around his waist under the backpack.) Have him don a secondhand muumuu and time him as he "runs" through the course. Award a prize to the pregnant papa who finishes the course in the shortest amount of time.

Pregnant Papas

→ Be prepared: this activity can get messy. Divide the players into pairs. Give one member of each pair a spoon and a small bowl of "baby food" (gelatin or pudding). Tie large bibs around the necks of the other members. Seat the bibbed team members and have the other members stand behind their partners. At your mark, the standing members must feed their partners. The first pair to finish the meal wins prizes.

Midnight Feeding

→ Write baby-related words on separate index cards. Seat the guests in a circle and give each a card. Seat the parents-to-be in the center of the circle. Have the guests take turns giving one-word clues that relate to the words on their cards. The parent-to-be who first correctly identifies the word from the provided clues wins that card. When all the cards have been won, the parent-to-be with the most cards wins.

Mama Versus Papa

→ This relay race is a great outdoor activity. Divide the guests into teams. Give each team member a filled water balloon. Have the teams line up, and have a "doctor on call" (the mom-to-be) seated at the finish line. At your mark, the first member of each team must race to the doctor with the water balloon between his or her legs. When a team member has dropped the water balloon in front of the doctor, the next team member begins the race with his or her water balloon. If a team member's water "breaks" along the way, provide another water-filled balloon and have him or her start the race over. Award prizes to the team that first delivers all its balloons to the doctor.

Race to the Doctor

→ Stage a Baby Bucks Auction. Photocopy the Baby Bucks on page 123 on blue or pink paper and cut out the Bucks. Use the following chart to award Baby Bucks to couples. Adapt the chart to suit your guests and include other criteria to award Bucks. For example, have the women leave the room and challenge the men to write down a description of the shoes their partners are wearing. Have the women return, and award $2 to each man who answered correctly. Once the Bucks are distributed, couples can use their Bucks to bid on inexpensive wrapped gifts.

✓ Award $1 for every year a couple has been married or has dated.

✓ Award $5 if the woman first asked the man out.

✓ Award $2 for each child they have.

✓ Award $5 for each child they had after age thirty (woman, man, or both).

✓ Award $20 if they're not married.

✓ Award $3 if they dated for more than three years before getting engaged.

✓ Award $1 for every poopy diaper changed within the last day.

✓ Award $1 for every 10 pounds gained during pregnancy. ("Empathy" weight gain counts.)

✓ Award $2 if they can provide the song title from the first dance at their wedding.

✓ Award $3 if they can remember the anniversary of their first date.

✓ Award $1 for every trip they or one of their children has had to the emergency room.

✓ Award $2 for every child they've successfully potty trained.

Baby Bucks Auction

Sip 'n' See

A typical Sip 'n' See is somewhat like an open house. Its primary goal is to spotlight the new arrival. The benefits of having a shower after the baby is born are three-fold. First, the guests can meet the little one at the party. Second, having many people meet the baby at one time will diminish the steady stream of visitors to the new parents' home over the first few weeks. And finally, guests can give gender-specific gifts. This kind of shower is also a perfect way to celebrate the adoption of a child of any age. The following is a list of considerations to keep in mind as you plan the celebration:

→ Wait to set the party date until after the baby's born. Give the new family at least a couple of weeks to recuperate after the birth before discussing party dates.

→ Keep the celebration brief. The new family needs rest and will fade quickly.

→ Serve a light buffet of appetizers along with beverages.

→ Activities are probably not necessary and might take the focus away from the wee one.

→ A photo of baby can be an ideal party favor. For example, see Baby Photo Plant Stakes on page 24 for a great photo favor idea.

→ You can adapt any party theme in this book for this type of celebration. For example, "A Star Is Born" (see page 93) might be the perfect way to commemorate the heavenly arrival.

Shower for a Faraway Friend

You can host a baby shower for the mom-to-be even if she lives miles away. In fact, a long-distance shower might be just what the doctor ordered for a pregnant friend who's feeling a little homesick or lonely during this exciting—yet sometimes overwhelming—time. Here are two shower ideas:

Baby Shower in a Box

→ A Baby Shower in a Box is a gift-wrapping extravaganza for guests that results in special delivery for the mom-to-be. Invite guests each to bring an unwrapped gift for baby. Along with snacks and beverages, provide lots of crafting supplies, like rubber stamps, stickers, stencils, tape, scissors, ribbon, markers, paint, and paintbrushes. Also provide rolls of plain newsprint, solid-colored gift-wrap, and brown craft paper. Have the guests take turns showing their gifts before the gift-wrapping begins.

As the gifts are wrapped, prop them around an oversized photo cutout of the mom-to-be. Take lots of photos of the festivities, and use a video recorder to film the party. If possible, plan to have the mom-to-be join you by speakerphone. Consider buying a decorative journal into which guests can pen congratulatory notes, well wishes, or parenting advice.

When the party's over, put all of the gifts, along with developed photos and the videotape of the celebration, in a large decorated box. Include a label on the box that reads, "Baby Shower in a Box: Open Contents Carefully and Enjoy!" Mail the box of goodies to the mom-to-be. You might also arrange to have a special cake sent to her so it arrives at the same time as the gifts. Many bakeries specialize in mail-order deliveries. Or have someone who lives close to the mom-to-be deliver a cake (prepaid by you) from a local bakery.

→ Schedule Twelve Days of Baby Shower. The goal of this baby shower, coordinated entirely through the mail, is to have the mom-to-be receive at least one gift every day for twelve days. In the "invitations," assign each guest a day on which she's to mail her shower gift directly to the mom-to-be. Or to more accurately gage the level of participation, ask guests to call you for their assigned dates.

If you like, mail a disposable camera and a list of all the guests' names and mailing addresses to the first guest on the list. Instruct her to snap a self-portrait (the funnier, the better), cross her name off the list, then send the camera and guest list within two days to the next guest on the list. Put your name as the last guest on the list so you can develop the photos. Send these photos to the mom-to-be so she can put a face to each gift.

Also consider assigning the guests each a theme for the gifts. A few examples of themes include play time, bath time, mealtime, and bedtime.

The Twelve Days of Baby Shower

SPRINKLE

This type of celebration is ideal for the mom-to-be who was showered with many big-ticket baby items when preparing for the births of her other children, but who could still use a sprinkling of baby essentials, like diapers or onesies. Or perhaps the mom-to-be still has loads of her son's baby clothes, but now needs to prepare for her newborn daughter's arrival.

At a sprinkle there isn't one itinerary to follow. You may choose to base the party on one of the themes in this book, but not include all components of the party. For example, you may decide to skip activities all together, opting instead for good conversation among good friends.

Since this celebration focuses more on the mom-to-be, consider giving gifts for her. They'll be especially welcomed by someone who already has at least one little one underfoot! You might invite each guest to bring a favorite frozen casserole to the party along with the recipe. At the party, provide blank recipe cards for guests who want to swap recipes. When the new baby arrives, the mom-to-be will certainly appreciate the readymade meals. (Make sure you have plenty of freezer space available to house the casseroles during the party, and warn the mom-to-be to clear her freezer, too.) Or provide a sign-up list at the party for guests to volunteer to deliver a homemade meal to the mom-to-be in the days after the baby's birth.

Or consider giving the mom-to-be a new pair of pajamas or a gift certificate to a favorite restaurant plus a "get out of the house free" card that offers your complimentary baby-sitting services.

SIBLING CELEBRATION

Giving up "only child" or "baby" status can be especially challenging for a family's first- or last-born child. Involving an expectant sibling in baby shower celebrations can help prevent sibling rivalry before it starts.

If the child is under the age of five, keep her involvement brief but lively. Have a basket filled with toys and other treats nearby, and consider hiring a baby sitter so mom can mingle even after the little one has tired of the party. (Make certain that the baby sitter is someone the child is comfortable with, or the plan will backfire.) The following are a few ways to make an expectant sibling feel included in the festivities:

→ Ask the child to draw a picture and have him sign the artwork. Make photocopies of the picture and use it in the invitations. Frame an invitation as a keepsake for mom.

→ Decorate a pintsize chair for the child to sit in next to mom.

→ Make a special T-shirt for her to wear to the party that reads, "I'm Going to Be a Big Sister."

→ Order a small cake made especially for him that reads, "Congratulations to the New Big Brother." Top the cake with candles. Let him blow them out and make a wish.

→ Invite each guest to bring a small gift for the sibling.

→ Ask guests to bring baby gifts that can involve the sibling. For example, give books that the child can "read" to baby. Present these gifts to the sibling in a child's backpack.

→ Choose at least one shower activity that the child will enjoy participating in. Or have the child team up with mom during activities. Note that pencil games may not be ideal, as young children can't read and older ones might find the activity too much like homework.

→ Unwrapping gifts is always fun for a small child. Try this gift-opening game. Fill a box with candy and wrap it in several layers of gift-wrap. Play a lullaby tape and have the guests, including the child, pass the gift around. Whenever the music stops, the guest holding the box unwraps one layer of gift-wrap. Play continues until the winner removes the last layer and shares the candy prize with the guests.

→ Give the child a disposable camera and make him the shower's photographer. When the photos are developed, it'll be fun for mom to see how the party looked from his perspective.

→ Make a "Big Sister" scrapbook in which the child can record the details of baby's arrival. Leave plenty of room for drawings.

Appendix

Recipes

Cutout Cake

2¼ cups flour
1 tablespoon baking powder
½ teaspoon salt
1⅔ cups sugar
¼ cup margarine, softened
1 cup milk
2 teaspoons vanilla extract
3 egg whites

Preheat your oven to 350°F. Sift the flour and baking powder into a mixing bowl. Add the remaining ingredients and blend until smooth. Pour the batter into a greased 13-by-9-inch cake pan (or two 9-inch round cake pans) lined with wax paper and bake for 35 minutes. Allow the cake to cool before removing it from the pan. For easier cutting and fewer crumbs, wrap the cake in plastic wrap and freeze it for 1 hour before cutting.

Basic Cake Frosting

6 cups powdered sugar
8 tablespoons milk
¾ cup margarine, softened
¼ cup shortening
1 teaspoon clear vanilla extract

Mix 3 cups of the powered sugar and 4 tablespoons of the milk with the margarine, shortening, and vanilla until smooth. Add the remaining powered sugar and beat until fluffy. Add the remaining

Cutout Cake

❦

Basic Cake Frosting

milk as needed to achieve the desired spreading consistency. This recipe makes 3 cups of frosting.

Frosting Tips

If using a disposable pastry bag, clip the bottom point of the bag and fit it with a decorative tip. To fill the bag, place it in an empty jar and fold the top edge over the jar's rim. You'll now be able to use both hands to spoon frosting into the bag. Add the frosting and twist the bag closed at the top to keep frosting from being squeezed out the top of the bag. Squeeze frosting through the tip of the bag to decorate desserts.

To make your own pastry bag, use a 1-gallon freezer-weight resealable plastic bag. Fill the bag with frosting and snip one of the bag's bottom corners. Press out any air from the bag, then seal it closed. Squeeze frosting through the cut corner.

Smooth Icing

3 cups powered sugar
¼ cup water
3 tablespoons light corn syrup
2 tablespoons margarine, softened
½ teaspoon clear vanilla extract
¼ teaspoon almond extract

Mix all the ingredients until smooth. Tint with food coloring if desired. Add additional drops of corn syrup to achieve the ideal spreading consistency. Keep the icing in an airtight container when you're not using it. This recipe makes 1½ cups of icing.

The Ultimate Sugar Cookie Dough

1 cup margarine, softened
1 cup sugar
2 eggs
3 teaspoons vanilla extract
4 cups flour
2 teaspoons baking powder
1 teaspoon salt

Mix the first 4 ingredients together until fluffy. Blend in the remaining ingredients. Wrap the dough in plastic wrap and refrigerate it for 2 hours. Preheat your oven to 375°F. Roll out a small portion of dough until it's ¼ inch thick (keep the rest of the dough refrigerated). Cut the dough into desired shapes and place them on greased baking sheets. Bake the cookies for 7 minutes or until the edges are golden brown. Cool the cookies on wire racks. This recipe makes 2 dozen 2½-inch cookies.

Chocolate Dessert Garnishes

Trace or draw the desired number of designs on a sheet of paper. (The less intricate the design is, the better. Always make a few extra garnishes in case some break.) Tape the paper to a baking sheet. Cover the sheet with wax paper and tape it in place. Melt equal amounts of semisweet chocolate and shortening over low heat. Stir the mixture constantly and don't let it overheat. Place the melted chocolate in a pastry bag with a writing tip (see page 116 to make your own bag). Trace the designs with the melted chocolate, making sure the lines are at least ¼ inch thick. Refrigerate the garnishes for 30 minutes to harden the chocolate, then peel the designs from the wax paper. Prop the finished garnishes against peaks of whipped topping on desserts.

The Ultimate
Sugar Cookie Dough

Chocolate Dessert
Garnishes

TEMPLATES

Pea Pod Template

Stork Gift Bingo Template

S	T	O	R	K
		FREE		

Pyramid Favor Box

This functional box can house anything from candy to flower bulbs. Use the provided template to cut boxes from decorative card stock. Score the box along the dotted lines. Punch a hole at the top of each corner. Bring the corners together and tie the box closed with a 16-inch ribbon. Lace one ribbon end through hole A and one end through hole B, bring both ends up through hole C, and tie the ends in a bow.

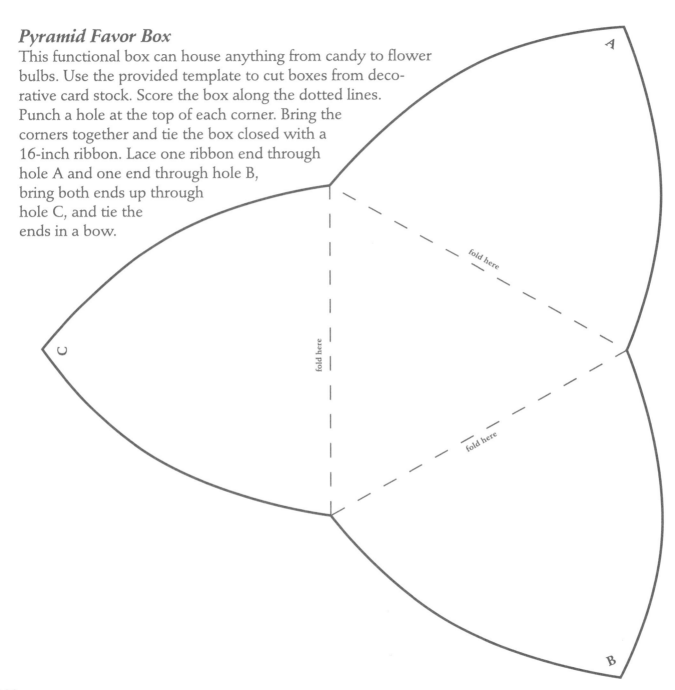

Baby Bucks

These bucks can be put to good use in the auction activity on page 108. If you like, before photocopying the bucks personalize them by taping baby photos of the parents-to-be or of the new arrival over the artwork.

GAMES

Mr. Stork's Special Delivery Quiz

Before reading the following list of questions to the group, give each player a sheet of paper and a pencil. Note that the mom-to-be will need to provide answers to the first five questions prior to the shower. (You can substitute the words *the mom-to-be* with her name.) The answer key follows the quiz. The player who gives the most correct answers is the winner. If a tiebreaker is needed, award the prize to the player whose birthday is closest to baby's due date.

1. When is the stork scheduled to visit the mom-to-be? (What's her due date?)

2. If the stork pays the mom-to-be a visit on this day, what will baby's zodiac sign be?

3. Help the stork out by providing the name of the street on which the mom-to-be lives.

4. When the mom-to-be was a baby, did the stork bring her before, after, or right on her due date?

5. On what date did the stork deliver the mom-to-be? (When's mom-to-be's birthday?)

6. Before the stork can arrive, a woman's cervix must completely dilate to how many centimeters?

7. Tell the stork what word the letter *C* in *C-section* represents.

8. The stork has how many lunar months to prepare for a baby's delivery? (How many lunar months are there in the average pregnancy?)

9. Please help the stork spell the word *episiotomy.*

10. Why are storks believed to deliver babies?

Mr. Stork's Special Delivery Quiz Answer Key

Answers to questions 1 through 5 are specific to the mom-to-be.
Here are the answers to the rest of the questions.

6. Ten
7. Cesarean
8. Ten
9. Episiotomy
10. The white stork is family oriented and gentle with its young. Each year these birds return in pairs to the same nesting spot.

Mother Goose Rhetoric

When the timer starts, have players write the exact first line of the
Mother Goose nursery rhyme that each phrase best describes.

1. Hungry girl afraid of bugs
2. On his way to becoming an omelet
3. Feathered dessert fit for royalty
4. A lady in a unique abode with boarders aplenty
5. Small boy gives pie a thumbs up
6. A bovine with lofty ambitions
7. Young shepherdess who misplaces things
8. Jumping lad with hot pants
9. Young window-peeping, time-keeping boy in pajamas
10. A trio of felines with cold paws
11. An elderly woman with canine who needs to go to the grocery store
12. Sleepy boy with musical instrument
13. Culinary gentleman who quickly prepares personalized pastries
14. Swift swine stealer
15. Klutzy couple on an uphill assignment

Mr. Stork's Special Delivery Quiz Answer Key

Mother Goose Rhetoric

Mother Goose Rhetoric Answer Key

1. Little Miss Muffet
2. Humpty Dumpty sat on a wall
3. Sing a song of sixpence
4. There was an old woman who lived in a shoe
5. Little Jack Horner
6. Hey, diddle, diddle!
7. Little Bo-Peep has lost her sheep
8. Jack be nimble, Jack be quick
9. Wee Willie Winkie runs through the town
10. The three little kittens
11. Old Mother Hubbard
12. Little Boy Blue, come, blow your horn!
13. Pat-a-cake, pat-a-cake
14. Tom, Tom, the piper's son
15. Jack and Jill went up the hill

Wright Family Story

The Wright Family lived in the second house on the right—right across the street from the grocery store. Mrs. Wright was expecting a baby right before Christmas. With one week left, Mrs. Wright decided it was time to get everything left on her list so she could have everything in the right order when the Wright baby arrived. Not feeling quite right, Mrs. Wright sent Mr. Wright to the store with the list. Mr. Wright put the list in his right hand and left for the store that was right across the street. Right before he got there, he slipped and hurt his right ankle. The man on his left helped Mr. Wright back to his feet. Mr. Wright thanked the man and then left to continue right on with his shopping. Once in the store, Mr. Wright found everything right where Mrs. Wright had told him it would be. The diapers were on the right side of Aisle One and the wipes were right below. The formula was right on the top shelf of Aisle Seven, which was to the right of Aisle One. The only thing left on Mr. Wright's list was a pacifier. He looked to the left of the formula and he looked to the right, but there didn't appear to be any pacifiers left, so he went home to check on Mrs. Wright.

Just as Mr. Wright walked through the door, he found that Mrs. Wright was ready to go right to the hospital to have the Wright baby. Mr. Wright left his packages right in the doorway and took Mrs. Wright by the right arm to help her right to the car. Mr. Wright made a right turn out of the driveway and drove fast, as Mrs. Wright thought Baby Wright might be coming right away. Mr. Wright drove to the intersection where you must yield the right of way to oncoming cars. Mr. Wright looked to his left, then to his right, and then raced on with Mrs. Wright on his right having contractions. He had to make one turn to the right, then one to the left and then one back to the right before reaching the hospital that was right across the street from the school. Just before they made their last right turn, Mrs. Wright realized that they had left her suitcase right by the door to the left of the closet. Mr. Wright assured Mrs. Wright he would return to get it after first getting Mrs. Wright to the right spot to have the Wright baby.

When the Wrights arrived at the hospital entrance, they were told to take a left, then a right, then a left, then a right before finding the labor and delivery area on their left. Mr. Wright checked Mrs. Wright in right away and then left to get the suitcase. Mrs. Wright was now holding her right side, confident that Baby Wright would be here very soon. And she was right; Mrs. Wright delivered the Wright baby right before Mr. Wright returned with the suitcase they had left behind. Now all was right for the Wrights who were left feeling overjoyed by their wonderful gift!

Wright Family Story

Who Wants to Be a Mommy?

1. In the story of "The Three Little Pigs," the third little pig escapes the wolf by building his house of what?

   a. Straw   c. Bricks

   b. Sticks   d. Vinyl siding

2. During which month will a baby usually sit up?

   a. Fourth   c. Ninth

   b. Sixth   d. Tenth

3. The term *cradle cap* most commonly refers to which of the following?

   a. A condition also known as *seborrheic dermatitis*

   b. A must-have fashion accessory in a well-dressed baby's layette

   c. The cap placed upon the newborn's head immediately after birth to help regulate body temperature

   d. A receded hairline on a newborn

4. According to a beloved poem, what ingredient are little boys not made of?

   a. Snails   c. Snakes

   b. Spice   d. Puppy dog tails

5. Which of the following folklores is said to foretell that you're having a girl?

   a. If you're 31 years old and conceive the baby in December

   b. If the baby's heart rate is 140 or above

   c. If the hair on your legs grows faster during pregnancy

   d. If you experience shortness of breath

6. How many points are possible on the Apgar score?

   a. Five   c. Ten

   b. Six   d. Twelve

7. On average, how many hours a day will the newborn sleep?

   a. Eight
           c. Twelve

   b. Ten
           d. Fourteen to eighteen

8. Doctor Foster is a Mother Goose character who did which of the following?

   a. Wore a velvet coat
           c. Got caught in the rain

   b. Went to St. Ives
           d. Jumped over a candlestick

9. What percentage of women deliver on their actual due date?

   a. 4 percent
           c. 12 percent

   b. 7 percent
           d. 16½ percent

10. What is meconium?

   a. A term used to describe a newborn's cone-shaped cranium

   b. A substance known to incapacitate Superman

   c. A type of mucus that may need to be extracted with an aspirator from the newborn's nasal passageway upon birth

   d. A tar-like substance that newborns excrete in their diaper the first few days of life

11. What practice contractions are named after an English doctor who first described them in 1872?

   a. Lamaze
           c. Braxton-Hicks

   b. Bradley
           d. Seuss

12. What is the average length of the umbilical cord at term?

   a. 18 inches
           c. 28 inches

   b. 21 inches
           d. 32 inches

13. *Engagement* is an obstetric term used to describe which of the following?

   a. The thinning of the cervix

   b. A cervix that's dilated to at least 1 centimeter

   c. A betrothal of the baby's parents

   d. The drop of the baby's head into the pelvis

*Who Wants
to Be a Mommy?*

*Who Wants
to Be a Mommy?*

*Who Wants
to Be a Mommy?
Answer Key*

Baby Doodles

Parent Speak

14. How many stages of labor are there?

   a. Three   b. Five

   c. Six   d. Too many to count

15. In the first three years of life, a child's brain will grow to what percent of its adult size?

   a. 33 percent   b. 50 percent

   c. 60 percent   d. 80 percent

Who Wants to Be a Mommy? Answer Key

1. c	5. b	9. a	13. d
2. b	6. c	10. d	14. a
3. a	7. d	11. c	15. d
4. b	8. c	12. b	

Baby Doodles

bottle	bib	blankie	potty chair
growth chart	rocking chair	teething ring	sunscreen
nipple	crib	bootie	bumper pads
swing	spillproof cup	breast pump	outlet covers
nasal aspirator	rattle	diaper	pacifier
pull toy	vaporizer	crib mobile	diaper pail
stroller	highchair	onesie	night-light
car seat	step stool	baby gate	puzzle

Parent Speak

On separate sheets of paper, draw blanks to indicate the number of letters in each word found in these classic phrases that moms and dads have been saying for decades.

1. Do you think money grows on trees?
2. Eat your vegetables!
3. Don't make me stop this car!
4. How many times do I have to tell you?
5. When I was your age…
6. Because I said so!
7. You'll poke your eye out!
8. Clean your plate!
9. Wash behind your ears!
10. What's the magic word?

Parent Speak

Pink & Blue Challenge

To provide material for both the pink and blue teams, have the
mom-to-be and the dad-to-be separately answer the questions.

1. What did the mom-to-be/dad-to-be weigh when s/he was born?
2. What is her/his birth date?
3. What is her/his middle name?
4. What was her/his first word?
5. What did s/he want to be when s/he grew up?
6. On whom did s/he have her/his first crush?
7. What color was her/his first car?
8. Provide the name of her/his high school mascot.
9. What year did s/he graduate from high school?
10. Where did s/he go to college?
11. Name one of her/his past roommates.
12. With what company has s/he been employed the longest?
13. Name one of her/his favorite hobbies.
14. What's the title of her/his favorite song?
15. What's her/his favorite color?
16. How did the expectant parents first meet?

Pink & Blue Challenge

Old Wives' Tales

Ask players to check their guesses for the following tests. Award a prize to the player who makes the most correct guesses.

1. If an expectant mom sits on the floor, then places her hands to her side rather than behind her to get up, she can expect a ❏ boy ❏ girl.

2. If an expectant mom stares into a mirror for at least one minute but no longer than three, and her eyes dilate, she will have a ❏ boy ❏ girl.

3. If a mom-to-be's left eye is brighter and left breast is bigger, it's a ❏ boy ❏ girl.

4. If baby prefers to kick the mom-to-be in the ribs, this baby is a ❏ boy ❏ girl.

5. By always carrying an onion in her pocket, the mom-to-be can guarantee a ❏ boy ❏ girl.

6. If you dangle a pencil over an expectant mom's wrist by sticking a threaded needle through the pencil's eraser, and the pencil swings from side to side, that indicates a ❏ boy ❏ girl.

7. A baby that sits on the right side of the womb is thought to be a ❏ boy ❏ girl.

8. If asked to show her hands and the expectant mom presents them with palms faceup, it's thought she'll have a ❏ boy ❏ girl.

9. A mom-to-be who complains of thinning hair should anticipate a ❏ boy ❏ girl.

10. If someone sprinkles salt in an unsuspecting mom-to-be's hair and she later begins to scratch her nose, she's going to have a ❏ boy ❏ girl.

Old Wives' Tales Answer Key

1. Boy	4. Boy	7. Boy	9. Girl
2. Boy	5. Girl	8. Girl	10. Boy
3. Girl	6. Boy		

Somebunny Famous

Have players race to unscramble these names of famous bunnies.

1. treep bitabr
2. srteea ybnun
3. hprmeut
4. het rhea dna eht rtsootie
5. gbus nbnuy
6. eprte ltnocioatt
7. yolbypa ynunb
8. erbr btirba
9. njmebian nyubn
10. eth elnetevve tabrib
11. atp eht nbynu
12. ltlite biratb oof ofo

Somebunny Famous Answer Key

1. Peter Rabbit
2. Easter Bunny
3. Thumper
4. The Hare and the Tortoise
5. Bugs Bunny
6. Peter Cottontail
7. Playboy Bunny
8. Brer Rabbit
9. Benjamin Bunny
10. The Velveteen Rabbit
11. Pat the Bunny
12. Little Rabbit Foo Foo

Hopping Down the Bunny Trail/Shake That Tune

These tunes can be used for either of these exciting activities.

"Mary Had a Little Lamb"　　　"The Wheels on the Bus"
"This Old Man"　　　　　　　 "The Alphabet Song"
"London Bridge"　　　　　　　"Twinkle, Twinkle, Little Star"
"Rock-a-Bye, Baby"　　　　　　"Row, Row, Row Your Boat"
"Hush, Little Baby"　　　　　　"I'm a Little Teapot"
"Jingle Bells"　　　　　　　　 "Old MacDonald Had a Farm"
"The Muffin Man"　　　　　　 "Where Is Thumbkin?"
"Hickory, Dickory, Dock"　　　 "Itsy Bitsy Spider"
"Frosty the Snowman"　　　　　"Pop Goes the Weasel!"
"The Hokey Pokey"　　　　　　"Happy Birthday"

Celestial Challenge

Team A	Team B
stargazing	astronaut
blue moon	stardust
man in the moon	UFO
astronomy	North Star
cyberspace	starfish
sunflower	meteor shower
star fruit	light years
"Twinkle, Twinkle, Little Star"	pearly gates
shooting star	angel food cake
head in the clouds	NASA
Big Dipper	space exploration
Capricorn	asteroid
star light, star bright	the cow jumped over the moon
heaven	Milky Way
Saturn	space suit

solar system	planets
angel hair pasta	sunset
constellation	*Star Trek*
cloud nine	starstruck
meteorology	movie star
seeing stars	lunar eclipse
moon rocks	Martian
crater	moonwalk
Star Wars	satellite

Celestial Challenge

Little Red Riding Hood's Basket

Goldilocks and the Three Bears	*The Three Little Pigs*
The Gingerbread Boy	*Henny Penny*
Cinderella	*The Three Billy Goats Gruff*
The Hunchback of Notre Dame	*The Prince and the Pauper*
Little Red Riding Hood	*The Little Red Hen*
Snow White and the Seven Dwarfs	*The House That Jack Built*
The Elves and the Shoemaker	*Jack and the Beanstalk*
Hansel and Gretel	*Puss in Boots*
The Princess and the Pea	*Rumpelstiltskin*
Beauty and the Beast	*The Emperor's New Clothes*
Rapunzel	*Alice in Wonderland*
Sleeping Beauty	*The Steadfast Tin Soldier*
The Frog Prince	*Pinocchio*
Peter Pan	*The Little Mermaid*
Aladdin	*Robin Hood*
Stone Soup	*King Midas*
Thumbelina	*Tom Thumb*
The Ugly Duckling	*Tarzan*

Little Red Riding Hood's Basket

Famous Story Lines

The object of this game is to be the first to identify the following tales from which these famous lines have been pulled.

1. "Fee-fi-fo-fum…"
2. "The night Max wore his wolf suit and made mischief of one kind and another…."
3. "'Not I,' said the goose. 'Not I,' said the cat. 'Not I,' said the dog."
4. "Who's that tripping over my bridge?"
5. "Mirror, mirror, on the wall, who's the fairest one of all?"
6. "And chances are if he asks for a glass of milk…"
7. "Then I'll huff, and I'll puff…"
8. "I'm late, I'm late, for a very important date."
9. "I do not like them, Sam-I-am."
10. "Somebody's been sleeping in my bed."
11. "I think I can…"
12. "In the great green room there was a telephone…"
13. "You can't catch me…"
14. "…that lay in the house…"
15. "Let down your hair."

Famous Story Lines Answer Key

1. *Jack and the Beanstalk*
2. *Where the Wild Things Are*
3. *The Little Red Hen*
4. *The Three Billy Goats Gruff*
5. *Snow White and the Seven Dwarfs*
6. *If You Give a Mouse a Cookie*
7. *The Three Little Pigs*
8. *Alice in Wonderland*
9. *Green Eggs and Ham*
10. *Goldilocks and the Three Bears*
11. *The Little Engine That Could*
12. *Goodnight Moon*
13. *The Gingerbread Boy*
14. *The House That Jack Built*
15. *Rapunzel*